DISILLUSIONMENT

DIALOGUE OF LACKS

DISILLUSIONMENT
From the Forbidden Fruit
to the Promised Land

David Gutmann,
François-Michel van der Rest,
Jacqueline Ternier-David,
and Christophe Verrier

DIALOGUE OF LACKS

David Gutmann and
Jean-François Millat

KARNAC
LONDON   NEW YORK

First published in 2005 by
H. Karnac (Books) Ltd.
6 Pembroke Buildings, London NW10 6RE

British Library Cataloguing in Publication Data

A C.I.P. for this book is available from the British Library

ISBN 1 85575 371 5

Edited, designed and produced by The Studio Publishing Services Ltd, Exeter EX4 8JN

Printed in Great Britain

10 9 8 7 6 5 4 3 2 1

www.karnacbooks.com

CONTENTS

To Charlotte and Sarah

CONTRIBUTORS

Guy Dollé, a graduate of the Ecole Polytechnique, was named Executive Vice-President of Usinor Aciers in 1986. Following the merger of Usinor Aciers with Sollac, Mr Dollé became head of production for the northern region of the new Sollac entity and was appointed vice-president, industrial affairs in November 1987. From 1993 to April 1995, he served as Chairman and Chief Executive Officer of Unimétal. He was then named Usinor Executive Vice-President in charge of strategy, planning and international affairs in 1995 and in 1997 became Head of the Stainless Steel and Alloys Division. He was appointed Senior Executive Vice-President of Usinor in 1999. After Usinor merged with Arbed and Aceralia, he was named CEO of Arcelor in 2002 and Chairman of Eurofer.

Dr Faith Gabelnick (1943–2004) was named president of Pacific University in 1995. She retired in 2003. Prior to 1995, Faith held teaching positions at the American University and the University of Maryland. She served as associate director of the General Honours Programme at the University of Maryland College Park, and as dean of the Carl and Winifred Lee Honors College at Western

Michigan University in Kalamazoo. In 1992, she accepted the post of provost and dean of faculty, and Cyrus B. Mills Professor at Mills College in Oakland, California. She was president of the A. K. Rice Institute from 1995 to 1997. Faith Gabelnick wrote several books and many book chapters, and was a frequent speaker at academic and professional meetings about her work, focusing on building and sustaining learning organizations, the role of women as leaders, and the study of leadership and institutional transformation. Faith served on many local and national professional and community boards, and she was Vice-President of the Northwest Health Foundation. She worked nationally and internationally as a consultant and director for institutes that study the psychodynamic, political, and radical aspects of leadership in organizations. She became, in October 2003, the Chair of the meetings of Praxis International Network.

David Gutmann is a graduate of the Institute of Political Studies in Paris, where he was Professor from 1990 to 1997, with a Masters degree in Public Law and a Doctorate in Political Sciences. He is currently Executive Chairman for Praxis International (Conseillers de Synthese/Advisers in Leadership), a company that he founded with Jacqueline Ternier-David in 1989. David Gutmann is also Executive Vice-President of the International Forum for Social Innovation, and Chair of the Organisational Consultancy Section and of the Governance and By-Laws Committee within the International Association of Group Psychotherapy (IAGP). An adviser for numerous leaders and managers of companies and other institutions in France and abroad, he is *maitre de conference* at l'Ecole Nationale d'Administration (ENA) and external professor and director of the programme "Leading Consultation" (Research Diploma, MPh, PhD) at the University of Glamorgan (Business School) in the UK. David Gutmann has also been awarded the French equivalent of knighthood (Chevalier de la Légion d' Honneur). During most of the 1980s, he took the role of staff member at the Leicester Conference (co-sponsored by the Tavistock Institute of Human Relations and the Tavistock Clinic) and continues to direct international conferences on the themes of Leadership, Institutional Transformation, and TransformAction throughout Europe, the Middle East, the West Indies, and the Americas. He is also a professional ski instructor. His first book *Psychoanalysis and Management: the Transformation* (Karnac, 2003) is also published in French, Italian, and Spanish.

Earl Hopper, Ph.D., is a psychoanalyst, group analyst, and organizational consultant in private practice. He is a supervisor and training analyst for the Institute of Group Analysis, the British Association of Psychotherapists and the London Centre for Psychotherapy. An honorary tutor at The Tavistock and Portman NHS Trust, and a member of the Post-Doctoral Programme at Adelphi University, New York, Earl Hopper is a past President of the International Association of Group Psychotherapy and a past Chairman of The Group of Independent Psychoanalysts of The British Psychoanalytical Society.

Jean-François Millat is a graduate of Ecole Supérieure d'Electricité in Paris. He made a career in Electricité de France and Gaz de France from 1968 to 2002. He has dedicated the rest of his career to management of human resources and industrial relations, partly as an expert and partly as a manager, partly at the corporate level and partly in the field. He has contributed to the internationalization of EDF and Gaz de France through creating the division preceding the present human resources departments of the two groups, especially through leading the negotiation that set up European Work Councils of EDF and of Gaz de France. He is now an independent consultant associated to Praxis International (Conseillers de Synthese/Advisers in Leadership). He has held various roles of staff member or director in international working conferences on the themes of Group Relations, Leadership, Institutional Transformation, and TransformAction throughout the world. Since 2002, Jean-François Millat is President of the International Forum for Social Innovation, and member of the International Association of Group Psychotherapy (IAGP).

Jacqueline Ternier-David is a Managing Director and Adviser in Leadership of Praxis International. She is a member of the Orientation Committee of the International Forum for Social Innovation; External Fellow of The University of Glamorgan, Pontypridd, UK; Permanent Faculty member of Leading

Consultation, and member of the International Association of Group Psychotherapy (IAGP). Jacqueline Ternier-David is a postgraduate in History at l'Université de Paris 1-Sorbonne, and in Business Administration at l'Ecole Supérieure d'Administration et de Direction des Affaires. She is also the author of *l'Entreprise dans la crise italienne* (Masson, Paris, 1982).

François-Michel van der Rest is a graduate in Philosophy and in Theatrical Sciences. He is actor, director, and consultant, chairman of Interest scrl, and administrator of Centre Sésame, an occupational centre for mentally handicapped people. He is also a member of the board of Fondation Internationale de l'Innovation Sociale-Belgique, and has worked on several occasions with Praxis International and IFSI.

Christophe Verrier is an Adviser in Leadership in Praxis International (Paris, France). A physician (MD), he practised medicine (humanitarian, GP, intensive care unit) before studying political sciences in Paris. He is also Visiting Fellow, The University of Glamorgan (Pontypridd, UK), a member of the International Association of Group Psychotherapy (IAGP), and member of IFSI. For this organization he has taken part, as a staff member, in various international working conferences in the Netherlands, Catalonia (Spain), the Palestinian Authority, Ukraine, Jamaica, UK, USA, Trinidad and Tobago, St Lucia, and Peru. He has directed these conferences in France since 2003.

Illusion . . . a word in the French language that results in many con-
tradictory definitions and uses, and that must not be confused with
dream or myth. Classical authors have often used it: from Flaubert
who "rarely experienced disillusions having had few illusions" to
Victor Hugo for whom "the soul has illusions, just as the bird has
wings, that is what supports him". Everyone has, or soothes oneself with, one's illusions; a physician is even capable of creating
optical illusions.

The analysis undertaken by the authors, who are also advisers
in leadership, is precise and systemic. It identifies the four original
illusions, or basic illusions, which shape themselves and develop
transitionally through intimate blending with counter-illusions.
They are neither good nor bad, but useful in our very genesis if the
adult occults them with force in his own unconscious, which has
become a safeguard keeping madness at bay.

Disillusionment, truly a process, is modelled in four clearly
characterized phases, which are both successive and closely intertwined: its final product, often temporary, in fact serves as a starting basis for a new form of illusion.

Illusions and disillusions are vital for the complexity of human nature or of an organization in reaching the Promised Land; "over-illusion" perhaps. We think we create illusions but in fact it is illusions that construct us.

Transformation, whether individual or collective, that is to say the changing of our mental representations, is anchored in disillusionment, which explains its often slow pace and difficulty. The evolution of the French steel industry and of Usinor, since the middle of the 1980s, provides an illustrative example. All the childhood illusions were tangled up in it: from omniscience to immortality, the downturn was always other people, i.e. primarily those "exotic" countries who exported at dumping price. We then implemented all the available means to show and convince our staff that in fact the downturn was us, through our incapacity to adapt to the environment! This transformation took several years, but from weeping spectators everyone then became actors in the process of change, through, in particular, the development of continuous improvement and participative management. Fifteen years later we are, through the creation of Arcelor, the world leader in our field . . . but aware of the limits and the threats of a new . . . illusion.

Guy Dollé
CEO (Chief Executive Officer) of ARCELOR
Arcelor: world leader in steel industry
(Président de la Direction Générale d'ARCELOR)
January 2004

FOREWORD

It is an honour and privilege to have been asked to write a Foreword to *Disillusionment* and *Dialogue of Lacks*, two very creative and evocative essays in the fields of social-psychoanalysis and group analysis in their deepest sense, disciplines founded on axioms that emphasize the sociality of human nature within biological, psychological, and socio-cultural domains. Although clarified and made relevant through interesting examples, these essays and their main arguments are highly abstract, and, therefore, constitute a perspective or meta-theory concerning a central theme of human development and group process, namely, "illusionment" and its vicissitudes, including "disillusionment", and "forms of instrumental adjustment" (Hopper, 1981) to the loss of the idealized object and perhaps of the good object as well. However, this theme continues to be neglected in both the Anglo-American and French literature. In fact, it is likely that both English and French are necessary in order to discuss these aspects of "la condition humaine" (Malraux, 1961). It is, therefore, hardly surprising that David Gutmann and his closest colleagues Francois-Michel van der Rest, Jacqueline Ternier-David, and Christophe Verrier have drawn on work from French and British psychoanalysis, journalism, fiction, poetry, and songs. They have done this both in order to situate their work within more general theories, to help make their main points, and to invite us to appreciate a particular nuance in their reading of the professional literature.

Informed by an awareness that man is always both subject and object, the basic project is the exploration of the contribution that illusions and their formation make to individual and collective consciousness, not dissimilar from the task undertaken by Huizinga (1970), the Dutch historian and sociologist, in *Homo Ludens*. Defining "illusion" in terms of its etymology in Latin, French, and Spanish, which is not really different from its etymology in English, and emphasizing its various connotations such as irony, deceit, mistake, and seduction, as well as play and hope, illusion is distinguished from fantasy, dream, myth, tale, and fiction, all of which are "lures" away from the mature appreciation of the Real and reality more generally. Recognizing that personal illusions are sometimes manifest in the illusions of institutions, and vice versa, the authors explore several complex illusions in the service of avoiding and circumventing the pain and suffering inherent in the recognition of loss, imperfection, and helplessness. With respect to the formation of illusions from the point of view of a model of normal and abnormal (pathological) personal development, the authors distinguish most interestingly between *major* illusions, concerning power, knowledge, and existence, and *transitional* illusions. The major illusions are those of omnipotence, immortality, and omniscience, all variations on and part of the underlying illusion of completeness, involving the true negation of lack.). Several transitional illusions are considered: beauty (or the aesthetic), permanence, individualism, possession, and castration. It is possible to consider many more transitional illusions, forged on the basis of attempts to make creative use of the debris of broken promises, both Real and imaginary.

The authors then ask the ultimate question: what makes it possible to stop being victims of illusion, to become free of its constraints, no matter how necessary and helpful some illusions may be, at least at some of the time and in some situations. A process of "dis-illusionment" is hypothesized, involving four phases, which are said to occur developmentally or epigenetically, as well as synchronically: unawareness, awareness, unconscious (deposition), and ultimate disillusionment. The process is said to proceed in an uneven and irregular manner, and is always partial. This section of the argument remains incomplete, but I agree with the authors' own point of view that this can be fruitful for further inquiry.

These essays conclude in a most suggestive way: the end and the beginning of them are merged in the metaphors and the concepts of "forbidden fruit" (of knowledge) and the "promised land" (of completion). T. S. Eliot would have approved. In other words, insight requires the process of disillusionment from illusionment that ultimate knowledge exists and it is possible to possess it. Reaching the promised land is impossible because it is located in the journey to it. Faust failed to appreciate one of God's two or three greatest jokes: by the time that many of us are ready and able to make creative use of the pain of disillusionment, it is time to die and to pass on the baton. We depend on successive generations as much as on preceding ones. However, this interdependence requires authentic dialogue among people and groups who represent and convey the disavowed and missing parts and qualities of one another. In other words, a renewed sense of completeness depends both on authentic dialogue across the generations and across the boundaries that define self and other, both personally and individually and with respect to social groups, for example, those of stratification, ethnicity, and gender. In this sense the cohesion of the self and the cohesion of the group depend on the successful negotiation of the process of disillusionment which gives rise to a more mature and realistic process of illusionment (Hopper, 2003a,b).

As might be apparent from these remarks, Gutmann and his colleagues have all been influenced: by the work of Marx, Weber, and Durkheim, the three Fathers of Sociology; by various schools of psychoanalysis, including the Kleinian, the Independent, and the socio-cultural orientations of Fromm and Horney; and by the work of Sartre and other Existentialist thinkers. Thus, we are encouraged to struggle to integrate essential ideas, and to acknowledge the importance of living with the tension inherent in the incomplete.

It is not without irony that I will conclude by reminding us that it was William Hazlitt, an early nineteenth-century Englishman, who observed, more or less *en passant*, that man is the only animal who both laughs and weeps, for he is also the only animal who is able, as far as we know, to perceive the difference between the way things are and the way they ought to be. We must now add that in the realm of human affairs both sets of perceptions, those of "are" and those of "ought", float on the Sea of Illusion. We must now acknowledge that the greatest challenge is to free ourselves from the chains of illusion while at the same time to toughen our souls. In this way we might better endure the pain that comes from the more complete appreciation of the Real. This is an essential step towards the development and maintenance of mature hope, defined as the ability and willingness to exercise the transcendent imagination concerning how we might make things better, not only for ourselves but also for those with whom we are in relationship and dialogue.

Earl Hopper, PhD

INTRODUCTION

No writing is innocent; it reflects, each time, not only its author's thoughts, but also his psychic state and the stages in his life, whether he is directly influenced by what is happening to him at the time of writing, or draws conclusions from what has been happening to him, or, even more strangely, is feeling or sensing intimately what is going to happen in his existence.

Neither of the two texts presented here escape this hypothesis. Of course, the second one is a continuation of the first, and could not have been written without it, but both together represent a crucial punctuation for me. *Disillusionment* is the result of a long and difficult reflection, with substantial periods of pause, a reflection that, in fact, has lasted for three years. Once the last full stop appended, the idea for the second text, *Dialogue of Lacks*, arrived very quickly, and was written on the back of it.

During this period, and particularly within the last few months, at the time of writing the *Dialogue of Lacks*, it is probably not by chance that I was confronted with a series of deaths of people close to me, in both my intimate life and my professional activity. My mother-in-law, Lotte Tenenbaum, died in her ninety-second year in September 2003; similarly, a friend and very dear colleague, Bruce

Reed, Lead-Consultant for the Grubb Institute in London, left us in November 2003. In both cases, their health and their age could allow us to envisage this fatal outcome. Conversely, Faith Gabelnick, past President of the A. K. Rice Institute, and one of our most eminent colleagues, as was Bruce, announced to us, early in December 2003, the diagnosis established by her doctors of pancreatic cancer. She had just turned sixty and retired from her job as President of Pacific University, to dedicate herself exclusively to her consultancy activity, including that within Praxis International Network. The shock and the suffering were thus even greater. Besides, I had invited her to comment on the texts that are presented to you; I had also asked Bruce, who had accepted, but had not been able to answer concretely, caught out by time . . .

The postscript concluding this book, which will probably remain Faith Gabelnick's last written work, makes its reading the more poignant and deep. Since then, the health of my own mother, a survivor of the Shoah, has suddenly deteriorated on her eighty-second birthday. The reader will undoubtedly understand that these texts, as "intellectual" as they might be, reflect an experience of life, and enable me, probably, to transform it into learning.

It is therefore not surprising that Praxis International Network decided, in the autumn 2003, that the New Year wishes that it sends to its partners would bear the theme of "Mourning". I think there can be no better conclusion to this short presentation, so here is my own text.

> The reader could rightly ask: why has Praxis International Network chosen such a theme for their New Year greetings card, which is supposed to open the way to the future, a future rich with promise and achievements? However, the theme for 2004 has never been so appropriate, even without any paradox, and we are now going to try to demonstrate this.
>
> Once again, the etymology will enlighten our reflection in referring to three different languages: French, English and Italian.
>
> The word *deuil* in French comes from the low Latin word *dolus*: pain. *Mourning*, in English, comes from the proto-Germanic *murnanan*, itself coming from the Greek *mermera* and the Sanskrit *smarati*, which all mean *memory* (*to remember*), a memory which acts with "care". In Italian, the word for mourning is *lutto*, the root of which, of course, evokes the struggle.

From the interaction of these three words, a new meaning and a new question emerge:

Mourning is pain, it is also memory, it is finally a struggle.

But why are we using the expression *travail de deuil* (literally "work of mourning")? It would appear as a process leading to overcome the pain of memory but mainly to transform the memory of the pain ... Thus the struggle is named: to not forget, to always pay attention to what (or who) has disappeared, but still to not let you be imprisoned by this pain.

Mourning is the result of a loss, most often the death of a dear one, more generally the loss of a relation (love, work, friendship), the loss of a mental representation, and of an affection.

Mourning, then, can be eminently destructive, even to the social link, leading to withdrawal into oneself, abandonment, and depression. For the Lacanians, it is like the symbolic castration and amputation. One would indeed say *"To lose a family member"*.

Thus, successful mourning, through a personal work helped by collective rituals, seems to make possible the transformation of a morbid memory, sometimes masochistic, even mortifying.

It does not avoid pain but becomes a struggle (*lutto*) for life, not for survival. It brings us out of the hold of the past and, starting from this loss, leads us to accept the lack. The lack which can itself generate desire ...

In our existence, to meet mourning can't be avoided. Moreover, it is a part of our humanity because it helps us to construct ourselves as conscious human beings. Conscious of our finiteness and thus, through this work of mourning, we are ready to live our lives fully, to build our future in the most useful, efficient and harmonious way.

David Gutmann
Paris, November 2004

DISILLUSIONMENT

Disillusionment

From the forbidden fruit to the Promised Land

David Gutmann, François-Michel van der Rest, Jacqueline Ternier-David, and Christophe Verrier

"Without the existence of desire, which founds the subject in the Real, life is an illusion"

Denis Vasse (1969), "Le temps du desir", *Le Seuil*, Paris

"We live most of the time behind screens. Veiled existences ..."

Francis Bacon in David Sylvester (1987), *Interviews with Francis Bacon*, Thames and Hudson.

"Illusion hides wrinkles and erases imperfection"

Advertisement, September 1999

We are all illusionists: we spend our life building, catching, touching, taming, and abandoning illusions. We let ourselves get caught by them. We attempt to catch others in the nets of our own illusions. That's how it is. And, just as for illusionists, it is they, these illusions, that make us exist, help us to construct ourselves, at the very same time as we construct them.

> Illusion suggests that one hides a part of things . . . indeed a magi-
> cian or an illusionist works with people's credulity, whereas I
> prefer to work with their intelligence or their curiosity [Markus
> Raetz, sculptor of "Metamorphoses", in *Liberation*, 6 August 2001]

The trudging that each of us is engaged in—over a shorter or
longer distance—while grappling with our own illusions is a
fundamental journey, intimate and unique, passing through our
own construction and touching on the very essence of our life. It is
not only about knowing whether we are being manipulated, or just
how far these illusions can obscure our judgement, our rational and
reasonable mind. Our freedom is at stake. It is about understanding
where the boundary lies between survival (and its frantic analogue,
all too frequent these days, that we refer to as "hyperlife") and a life
of desire and creation.

> Psychoanalytic practice is based on the bringing to awareness of the
> constant work of a Death force: the one that consists in killing the
> wonderful (or terrifying) child who, from generation to generation,
> brings testimony to his parents' dreams and desires; there is life
> only at the price of murdering the strange, primary image into
> which the birth of each of us is inscribed. An unrealisable murder,
> but a necessary one, for no life is possible—life of desire, life of
> creation—if one doesn't continue to kill the "wonderful child"
> forever reborn. [Serge Leclaire (1975), "On tue un enfant", *Le Seuil*,
> Paris, 1975]

Our intention here is to formulate a starting hypothesis and to
begin to unfold it in order to discover its consequences. It is based
on our experience as advisers in leadership which invites us to
work regularly with this kind of questions with leaders of organizations. Illusion is indeed as much an individual issue as it is a
collective and institutional one. The hypothesis is as follows: *we
believe that we construct and create illusions; in fact, it is they who
construct us.* And they do this in a very particular alternating movement, a waltz or a two-phase engine, a sinusoid's pulse, a yin and
a yang, a big and a bang, a zig and a zag, a specific Breathe in . . .
Breathe out! that goes: *illusion . . . disillusion!*

Our aim is to grasp the nature of these illusions from a few
concrete examples, borrowed as much from the personal field as
from the institutional one, and then to understand how these

illusions work, as well as the nature of the processes that they generate throughout our life. Finally, we will examine how, through confrontation with desire and lack, we can recognize (and therefore be reborn from) our own illusions, one after the other.This journey, the *disillusionment* process, is often long and tortuous. It erupts sometimes like a revelation and can enable each of us to apprehend reality in a more adjusted, maybe even more lucid, manner; to stop existing under the stronghold of our "systems-in-the-mind",[1] our mental representations, so as to benefit, in our individual life as much as in that of our institutions, from a relative freedom, the taste and content of which are suddenly renewed.

The stake

The flower of illusion produces the fruit of reality. [*Paul Claudel Journal, Tome 1, 1904–1932,* Gallimard, 1990]

At first glance, three attitudes are possible. Each of us can act because he is, without his knowing, the victim of an illusion. Whether he is prisoner, or even victim of this illusion, or whether he is complaisant towards it, this illusion orientates (or, in fact, disorientates!) his judgement and his discernment while sometimes bringing to him energy for action.Others have become aware of the illusory aspect of everything. At least of what has enabled them to live for many long years. They have "lost their illusions".[2] So now they need to discover what they are going to do for the rest of their existence.The third attitude is a mix of the first two: at times subject, at other times object, of illusion, they partly recognize what manipulates them. And they oscillate between *laisser-faire* and taking responsibility, despair and hope, confusion and discernment. This basic classification is not limited to individuals. Our intent is to broaden it out to social groups, or, more precisely, to human systems, be they nations, institutions (companies, public sector organizations, etc.), or small groups (family, society).

The nature of illusions

Why do we entertain illusions? Because we are human beings. There is no boundary and no frontier guard to erect barrages to our fantasies, our illusions, our hopes, our aspirations, our utopias, our hallucinations. These are contiguous pieces of land. In the no man's land zones, they play a game of trading places, just like ghosts, in the night, enjoy circle dancing. [Duong Thu Huong, in *Liberation*, 14 October 1999]

Each of us constructs illusions as we develop our own psychic life. They erupt from the meanders of this psyche and its procession of desires, fantasies, beliefs, convictions, assumptions . . . They distort our representations of reality and obscure our reasoning. They get in the way of our discernment and are capable of inhibiting our capacity for action or, conversely, of inviting us to take disproportionate risks: they "take us for a ride", and what a dangerous ride it can be . . . However, this darkness, this distortion, this obstacle, this inhibition that illusions can produce on our perception and on our understanding of reality are not all negative. *It is as if it was inevitable and even necessary to be taken for that ride, at least for a while.* If not inevitable, could the illusion be necessary? The issue here is not to denigrate illusions, but to explore their essential contribution to the construction of both individual and collective consciousness.

Defining illusion

Illusion is a word borrowed, circa 1120, from the classical Latin word *illusio*, meaning *irony* in rhetoric, linking it to *interrogation*, to the *act of interrogating whilst feigning ignorance*, in other words, to the method that Socrates used, while questioning his interlocutors, to thwart the condescension of some of them and uncover their ignorance (*Eironeia* comes *from eiron, -onos: he who interrogates whilst pretending to be ignorant*).[3] This first historic definition helps us get an inkling of what an illusion is. Indeed, condescension can only be the behaviour of someone in the midst of an illusion of wide knowledge, even maybe of complete knowledge (the illusion of omniscience referred to later on). What is referred to here is a conviction linked to the internal life of Socrates' interlocutor, which comes to influence his rooting into reality by inviting him to be condescending. Hence the value of the Socratic method as a way of revealing the part of ignorance and of helping the interlocutor recognize and unmask the illusion that manipulates him. In Christian Latin, *illusio* takes the meaning of *mockery, object of derision*, but also of *mistake in meaning, deceit, mirage, disappointment*. In fact, *illusio* is derived from the supine *illudere: to make a game of, to not care* about something, made from *il-* (marking negation) and *ludere*, meaning *playing*. In French, circa 1223, *illusion* refers to a *false appearance, an error in perception of which it is the cause (optical illusion)* and, circa 1611, in a more abstract way, *a wrong opinion forged by the mind, and which abuses by its seductive character*. It is the meaning of such utterances as *with no illusion, to cherish illusions, to be under a (de)lusion*.Finally, in Spanish, a second meaning can be added to the word *ilusión*: one of joy, of happiness, but also of hope.[4] Therefore, through these three characteristics—a mistake (a misleading representation of reality), virtuality (a psychic production), and manipulation (the individual is the victim of an illusion)—illusion is constructed *from the Real* of which it gives an erroneous representation—if not to say *ironic*. In the midst of illusion, I am the object, and not the subject, of the game. If I don't play the game (of the Real), I become the toy in the game, I lose my "I" status. The illusion is an *a-temporal some-where else* into where I project and transfer myself, which takes me away from the *here-and-now* of the game and of the I. *Illusion is therefore different from fantasy, dream, myth, tale, or fiction.*

> Our era prefers the image to the thing, the copy to its original, reproduction to reality, appearance to being. [Feuerbach]

> The extreme fondness of the human mind for falsehood forever holds surprises. [Hans-Georg Gadamer]

Myth, from the Greek *muthos*, refers to "a series of words which have meaning". A myth is a discourse organized in the same fashion as a fictional account. In other words, it can give reality an increase in meaning and new opportunities for interpreting it. It is as if it created a synthesis of interpretations of this reality through the medium of fiction. Through successive transformations, a myth is constructed from an old reality, whether it existed or was invented. It is concerned more with a collective group than with an isolated individual.

> If it is so dangerous, from the depth of our night, to catch a glimpse of light, one might as well try to approach it through myths,

Plutarque would suggest ... [...] Are mythical, for me, all the
legends, the stories, the works and the individuals that forge our
unconscious, both individual and collective. [Pietro Citati, "We
need myths to remain human": interview by Fabienne Pascaud for
Telerama 2561, 10 February 1999]

Close to the myth, we have the *tale*, which, similarly, delivers a
meaning about our very existence through an often very simple
content.

[...] I had to resort to more primitive, more original forms. With
humans, it is myth. Before humankind, with animals, it is dream.
[...] Then comes a tale, or myth—I do not differentiate between the
two—which consists of sequences of events told as simply as possible, and which are situated upstream from the first person, from
the constitution of the subject, from an autobiography. [Pascal
Quignard, "Lucidity means giving up believing that what we say
is true": interview by Michele Gazier for *Telerama* 2747, 4 September
2002]

For every myth there is a counter-myth that opposes it. For
example, to the principle of Good echoes a principle of Evil (God/
Devil, angel/demon). Through these counter-myths, God gives
space; retires from the world to allow the exercise of relativity. In
contrast, an illusion tends to remain within the realm of the unfor-
mulated, "stuck" to the very process of the perception of reality. To
apply the idea of myth to an organization or an institution implies
that we hypothesize that it can construct, from its history, a statement that it will pass on from generation to generation, within its
social body, contributing in that way to giving a general meaning to
its life and its daily activity and to reinforcing its cohesion.[5] We
know, however, that today one of the most recurrent problems for
institutions is the pace at which their environment constantly trans-
forms, and the fact that this demands from them, in return, a capacity to transform at least as rapidly. In that context, what weight do
institutional myths such as the kinds we have just outlined still
have? It seems that the founding myth could evolve into a series of
secondary myths, matching the development of the institution's
transformation. Similarly, in the creation of a certain number of hi-
tech start-ups, the myth that generates these companies could be

derived from the dominant myth of our capitalist society: to succeed very quickly when you've started from nothing, just like the . . . mythical figures of American capitalism at the turn of the century. This myth hinges on the illusion of believing that one has imagined something perfect, that one has thought of every little detail, thus giving in to the illusions of omnipotence and omni-science (see below). The risk then is to worry more about a theoret-ical model than about reality as it is; to imagine a planned trajectory and forget that this planning remains hypothetical, that the way through will reveal itself to be very different to what it had first looked like; and to consign the surprise inherent to any realization to the status of *unpleasant* surprise, unpleasant because unforeseen. This illusion derives from the very nature of the hi-tech product: technology is based on the fantasy of an absolute sovereignty of machinery over human fallibility, the only obstacle to perfect and totalitarian planning. We can see here an obliteration of reality, a magic belief in the infallibility of the technical tool's material components. Does the head of the start-up not run the risk, in that context, of placing himself in a position of semi-god and of want-ing to incarnate imaginary gods (Rockefeller, Bill Gates, etc.) of a Faith[6] based on quick money? This Faith itself may even be based on the illusion of infinite material progress, which is not character-istic only of capitalism, and which can be linked to the image of a maternal breast that could provide for every need.Further down the line, isn't there a danger of getting carried away, of an illusory "always-more"? Out of a thousand start-ups, how many are successful, and for how long? The creation of a start-up relies as much on what we could call the "Las Vegas syndrome".[7] It is like a jackpot, the illusion of finding a way of making a fortune, while we know that jackpot is a zero-sum game. Mirage of an arid land trans-formed into an oasis at the throw of a dice, a start-up then becomes a construction of the mind, a "modelling" that constantly runs the risk of hitting its teeth on reality—reality being always more power-ful than the imaginary. . . .[8]

The *dream*[9] has a very close relationship with illusion: when we dream, we are in total illusion, since we believe that what we are dreaming about is reality. Starting with the lived perception during waking state, a dream re-assembles life (through the play of associ-ations, contractions, displacements). A dream can be told, put into form and into words. It can be placed at a distance (even if, when it appears, this distance is minute). In that way, a dream can be made conscious. A dream, and especially its analysis, can give way to the revelation of an illusion. Myth and dream have in common the fact that both can be told: in this "becoming a story", the contents of a myth and of a dream evolve, get transformed. In that way, both call for interpretation. Myth and dream tell the movement of to-and-fro between different ways of seeing reality. Their account, when reality is put into fiction, reveals the difference of outlooks placed on this reality. We could argue, therefore, that interpretation is co-substantial to dream and myth, because they reveal the eruption of the Other, of what could not be integrated into the Conscious but was recorded or produced by the Unconscious. But whereas a dream, during its passage into consciousness (through all types of interpretation, including psychoanalysis), can renew meaning, an illusion, by contrast, resists this passage into consciousness. That is not to say that an illusion is invincible or indiscernible, but that maybe it is situated in an other realm. As if an illusion were a mix of conscious and unconscious that have become locked into each other. An illusion does not imagine that there could be any distance. The case of *fantasy*[10] is more complex. In contrast with illusion, fantasy is a production of the imaginary based on reality, but as a way of avoiding it. It is so that we can escape the stronghold of that reality that we construct fantasy, which is, in itself, the unconscious construction of a reality that is other.[11] However, if a fantasy is over-present, or too much shared, it can become a collective illusion: it misleads by putting up a screen between the subject and reality. The possible closeness between fantasy and illusion also invites us to cast a different, less black-and-white look on illusion. Even if fantasy and illusion mislead—at least in part—our representation of reality, both can in some cases be very useful when they enable us to go forward and to create. More precisely, one ought to acknowledge the mobilizing dimension of some fantasies, which pushes us to action, at least temporarily. Such is the case for business projects, which make it possible for the social body to move forward. Everyone knows the discrepancy between the initial project and the achieved result. However, the project was still able to stimulate a real mobilizing energy. Similarly, the example of the European construction is a wealth of transitory fantasies—the coal–steel pact, the Defence European Community, the Schengen Space, the single currency maybe—which, despite their partly fantasy-like nature, made it possible to achieve crucial milestones in the creation of binding links between Europeans. Thus, certain fantasies can be thought of as "transitional", when they are able to trigger the bridging towards the new stage of an on-going process. *Fiction*[12] is the archetype of transitional illusion. Telling (himself) stories, inventing stories (for himself) is a way for the individual to place himself in front of reality, while purposefully distorting it, re-assembling it into an account, and allowing his imaginary and his unconscious to speak up.

> . . . The so-called witness accounts on which ["positive" History] is based do not escape the falsifications ordered by the desire to be right. Fiction does not aspire to any objective accuracy, it is there-fore even freer in its movements: better equipped in any case to approach, as closely as possible, the ungraspable truth.[13]

Fiction uses forms that get round censorship, by making accept-able the Unconscious's content and "monsters". Fiction can act as a metaphor for a situation, in order to apprehend it differently, as a way of bringing out its hidden or invisible traits. As Wim Wenders writes:

> in reality, I believe that stories are lies; but [. . .] stories are very very very useful as forms of survival. Stories are an artificial structure which helps men conquer their greatest fears: fear that there might not be a God, and that they may only be fluctuating elements with the gift of perception, lost in a Universe that transcends every one of their imaginations.[14]

Taking apart an illusion by constructing representations (which could be understood as illusions under control) is one of the resources that man has been giving himself since his origin to better understand reality, by shifting it. With regard to illusion, what might we have learnt from this brief exploration of the issues of myth, dream, fantasy, and fiction? All are psychic processes which, beyond their differences, are connected by their capacity to consti-tute *lures*[15] for the human psyche, and in that way move it away from reality. Perhaps each of us chooses more readily one way of being lured rather than another, depending on the nature of one's own psychic dispositions. As far as illusion is concerned, the latter is silent, perhaps even mute; it censors the expression of the imaginary and, more importantly, of the unconscious. It leads us to believe that there is one and only one reality. It blinds us and flabbergasts[16] us. It is fascinating and fascizing, in the primary meaning of the word: it gathers into fasciculus evidences from reality in order to jugulate it. Illusion demands obedience and submission. We could thus be tempted to perceive the Roman Catholic dogma of pontifical infallibility in that way. Illusion wants to be reality. It is totalitarian and cannot imagine any placing at a distance. It cannot admit the Other. Illusion repeats itself without interpretation: it is just blind mimesis, in contrast to myth, dream, fantasy, or fiction, which all call in some way for interpretation. In illusion, there is only oneself, there is only sameness.

Personal illusions, institutional illusions

In order to make more audible what the work of illusion represents in institutions and the links between personal illusions and institutional illusions, we would like to refer here to three examples:

Mourning (accepting the death of the other)

Mourning reveals itself to be both a challenge and an illusion. At the individual level, the death of a close one gives birth to the illusion that life without him/her is impossible. Beyond the pain and the sorrow, it is a way of taking that death on to ourselves. What, indeed, can it tell us about our own death? To refuse the death of the other seems to maintain us in an illusion of immortality. A grieving process consists in turning down a halfway state between life and death. To grieve is to unmask the illusion of infinite life, of a life that would not be bordered by the intangible boundaries of birth and death. It is about admitting one's own temporality. It is about accepting life in its most absurd dimension, its most tragic one—death is one part of life—and, consequently, continuing (or restarting) to live a man's life—and not one of a semi-god, or a less-than-human . . .

> For the subject, mourning as loss is a hole in the Real, and possesses this traumatic dimension of an encounter with the Real. [. . .] The

term mourning covers two distinct elements. On the one hand, the loss of an object as such, and on the other hand, the mourning process linked and caused by this loss. [Jean-Marie Forget, "Mourning and castration during adolescence": extract from an internal working document for the limited audience of the members of the International Freudian Association, and with a special feature on J. Lacan: "Desire and its interpretation"]

But to mourn supposes also that one learns to be "sufficiently" sufficient to oneself, to manage to be both the child and the adult that protects it.

The mourning process enables one to both realise that one is alone and to get used to this loneliness, but also to understand that this loneliness is as much amputation as it is acknowledgement of the imperative necessity of the Other to prevent loneliness from turning into isolation.[17]

We come across this mourning process in institutions too. It is the case for companies in the midst of a situation of succession: the whole institution can deny reality by refusing the founder's or, more generally, the predecessor's physical or psychic disappearance and in seeing in the successor only a clone of the previous one. By jumping with both feet and with complaisance into the illusion of an immutable, or even immortal company, these employees refuse to mourn the founder, but also the possibility of transformation for the institution. And, consequently, its potential perenniality.

With one of our partners, a family business, the succession process was suddenly kick-started when the founding lady died. Everything, in the company's premises, still oozes of her presence (omnipresent image, systematic reference to "what she would have wanted", to the values that she has suggested for the company). Everything happens as if the deceased still occupies her seat: her ghost haunts everybody's mind. She has become the statue of the commander.

However the deceased president is now being replaced by her own daughter. Violent fantasies of fusion and unity are then projected on to mother and daughter as if they were one and the same person. In that context, what level of authority still remains available to the new president? Will the system, locked into a perpetual past, authorize her to become something other than a parody of her mother, than a chimerical and mimetic reproduction of the image of an eternal leader? However, if the institution did recognize its psychic dependence *vis-à-vis* the image of a dead woman, it would become possible for it to leave its morbid representation of reality and return in the here-and-now. The disillusion here hinges on the acknowledgement of a carefully dodged fact: leaders, however charismatic they may be, are neither eternal gods, nor invincible superhumans.

Not to acknowledge this fact, not to work through the mourning process, leads to refusing separation and to cutting oneself off from resources that it could bring, starting with the search for one's own authority. It means locking oneself up in a fantasy-like representation of the system which is based on *castration anxiety*. Because castration is aimed at preventing reproduction, it is clearly the fear of seeing the system's perenniality threatened that this is about. This anxiety leads us to consider the system as one and multiple, indivisible and immortal (the traditional attributes of divinity).

> We mourn and we feel the devaluing effects of mourning for as much as the object that we are mourning was, without our knowing, the one that had made themselves, that we had made, the support of our castration. [Jacques Lacan, seminar on Anxiety, quoted by Jean-Marie Forget in "Mourning and castration during adolescence": extract from an internal working document for the limited audience of the members of the International Freudian Association, and with a special feature on J. Lacan: "Desire and its interpretation"]

Castration anxiety thus generates an illusion of immortality for both the individual and the institution. By contrast, accepting separation, amputation, and castration enables us to understand—not only in an intellectual manner, but also in an emotional one—that we are incomplete, that we are not the whole, that we are partial. In fact, castration and mourning describe the same process: the loss of a member! Whether this member is the real, imaginary, or symbolic phallus, or whether it is a member of our own family or of any other institution, each time this loss, this lack, this emptiness, enables us to recognize our imperfection in order to fight it relentlessly while knowing very well that fortunately it will never be repaired. Separation is not fought through reparation. By contrast, if it is allowed to go on, this illusion halts any relationship between people and institution. This rigidity renders impossible any transformation, and any transformation of roles: if the individual–leader cannot be differentiated from the institution, he/she loses their status of ephemeral human being and becomes an image, divine or supernatural (and therefore untouchable and non-transformable). Thus, the institution itself becomes untouchable and non-transformable. And the only possibility left is radical destruction: what cannot be passed on must be destroyed, at the risk of self-destruction.

Perfection (a God amongst men)

Let us take a second example borrowed from institutional life: the perfect director; an illusion in the institution.

> During one of our consultancy experiences, everyone in the company was convinced that the director was perfect: of a competence greatly superior to that of his colleagues, and of an unequalled intelligence. This illusion, shared by the director himself, was one of the major characteristics of the representation of the system that organizational members had constructed. From then on, the internal life of the company was organized around it. The director, caught up in the vicious circle of his colleagues' projections and of his own fantasies, was locking himself up in an all-powerful posture. As for the other members of the institution, they were tying themselves up in games that mixed stronghold, contempt, and envy, fighting constantly to get close to the director (while, however, never daring to challenge him, not even in a constructive competition). We have called this stage a *"sideration" block.*[18]

This example, just like the previous one, shows how an illusion can influence, maybe even organize, the life of a whole institutional system. It sentences that system to processes of repetition, in which the illusions of some get reflected, in a mirroring effect, in those of others. The system grinds to a halt, so that it ends up incapable of escaping such a homeostasis, and even more incapable of transforming itself. In this example, in collusion with his colleagues, the director is prisoner not only of an illusion of omnipotence, but also of an illusion of immortality (see below). The observations of such a situation tend to confirm the hypothesis, already alluded to somewhere else,[19] that organizations are created in response to their founders' fantasy: that their organization will outlive them or even keep them alive, and, therefore, enable them to escape their own death. Acknowledging the ineluctability of his physical or professional disappearance would have enabled this director to understand how much his company needs a process of generativity that could then offer him the opportunity of preparing for his succession, an essential prerequisite to institutional perenniality.

The European construction (a disillusion process between states)

> In approaching the twentieth century, the last one of the millennium, Europeans are convinced that they are at the *avant-garde* of civilization. Culture, intellectual refinement, artistic and literary blaze, unprecedented technological and industrial development, construction of philosophical and ideological models never, hitherto, so powerful: Europe glows with pride for its development. It also repeats, since the dawn of civilization right through Ancient Greece and Imperial Rome, a fantasy-based vision of its situation: one of an island of civilization lost in an ocean of barbarism. In the name of this vision, Europe had previously embraced colonial expansion and religious proselytism. The atrocities of the two World Wars, and of the Second in particular, give this illusion its *coup de grace*. Europeans suddenly discover, quite brutally and with clear evidences, that barbarism is not outside Europe, but very much within it; that it is among one of the most "fairly" distributed things in humankind; that every man, even the most "civilized" one, is a potential barbarian.[20] Suddenly, the split off—and cumbersome—part of human nature comes back in a most savage way!Thus, 1945 marks the end of a powerful illusion: brought down from its self-proclaimed title of model for the most perfected human being (in other words of all-round man, civilized man), the European is naked. He is beginning to understand that he shares with his fellow men a similar human condition. One cannot but acknowledge also that it is at the precise moment when this disillusion erupts that Europe truly engages in the construction of the European union, under the banner of "No more war!" Relationships between states go, not always so smoothly, from rivalry to co-operation and collective construction. We highlight this concomitance not as an expression of mere chance, but as the result of a process: leaving the realm of illusions (*avant-garde* of civilization, idealized culture, etc.), Europeans can at last get a grip on reality, and once again have their feet on the ground. From then on, they can, by unveiling their humility, envisage the future in a

transformed and, this time, constructive manner. In this example, let us remember that the end of illusions can constitute the starting point for a process of construction and creativity even if that process, as we will see later on, is not free of either regressions, or blocks.Of course, contemporary history could give us many other examples. What can we say about the illusion of invulnerability in which Americans regularly bathe, from Vietnam right through to Afghanistan, including the Bay of Pigs?[21]

Genesis

Our hypothesis has led us to think that the construction of personality, since early childhood, comes across one original illusion and three major illusions laid down on life's journey like necessary passages for the achievement of certain milestones. Each of us comes across these illusions, experiments with them, and then, in the best of cases, recognizes them and accepts them as illusions in a disillusionment process. These illusions—which bear on relationships to the issues of *power*, *knowledge*, and *existence*—can then combine to give birth to transitional illusions, those that make it even more possible for us to grow, mature and transform.

Major illusions

By major illusions, we refer to those that mark the rhythm of development for the young human being, and that provide, through combining with one another, the foundations for the following three major illusions of adult life come from one unique and original illusion: the illusion of completeness. We will in turn look at the major illusions of omnipotence, immortality, and omniscience.

Omnipotence

> [. . .] we are such stuff
> As dreams are made on; and our little life
> Is rounded with a sleep . . .
> [William Shakespeare, *The Tempest*, Act IV, sc. 1]

By evoking the most intimate processes of envy and gratitude from the very first hours of life, Melanie Klein[22] describes these two drives as the most active ones in the infant at a time when the foeto–maternal unity comes to an end. This moment is also an opportunity for the discovery of a mother who is separate from his own body.

> A mother's adaptation to the needs of her infant, when that mother is 'good enough', gives the infant the illusion that an external reality does exist that matches his own capacity to create. [D. W. Winnicott (1953), *Transitional Objects and Transitional Phenomena, A Study of the First Not-me Possession*]

In the first instance, the infant might feel himself to be omnipotent when his crying, his wailing, and his screaming lead him, in the best of cases, to obtain the satisfaction of his most elementary needs: "I cry therefore I can!" But soon, his mother escapes him: she acts according to her own will (her good will?) and appears to be holding all the power since only she is capable of relieving his primary frustrations: hunger, solitude, feeling of transitory neglect, and so on. Thus, the all-powerfulness becomes external to the infant, to his own being. He discovers that almightiness, in other words the capacity to control the world around him, is just an illusion.

> The ultimate task of the mother is to progressively disillusion the infant, but she can only hope to achieve this if she has shown herself capable of giving sufficient possibilities for illusion. [D. W. Winnicott, *ibid.*]

Having said that, this fantasy of almightiness might not be linked solely to this physical discontinuity that comes up and separates two bodies. The mother, too, experiences this rupture with great suffering (as shown at times with post natal depression). Maybe she projects on to the infant feelings of regret for this fusional period that she has lived with the foetus over the previous nine months. In any case, only lack makes it possible to come out of this illusion. Lack, loss, absence of the mother, enable the infant to come out of this fusion–confusion that is close to madness. More often this occurs with the help of the father—symbolic or real—who works at creating other links with the real, thus taking part in the rupture of this fusional link. One of the possible consequences of this first disillusion is the necessity to find words that can speak those new and all-so-strange feelings. It is the acquisition of language that soon makes of this very young child a speaking being.

> The one we lost is our first world. We are two-phase creatures. The first phase, the first world, the nine month spent in the mother's womb, is lost forever the day we are born. The only link that remains between the first and the second world is the soprano of the maternal voice. That is how we are constructed. "I think that we had a real experience when we could not talk". This statement, to which I wholly subscribe, is not by Françoise Dolto but by Saint Augustine. We had, before we acquired language, around the age of twenty months, a real deciding, concentrated auditory experience. It is that very same experience that we can find in silent reading or in writing. An experience with our eyelids half shut. We bring back to experience an internal state. A former state. [Pascal Quignard, "Lucidity means giving up believing that what we say is true": interview by Michele Gazier for *Telerama* 2747, 4 September 2002]

Thus, the relationship that we have, throughout our life, with the illusion of almightiness may well depend on these first few moments. The illusion of omnipotence is still there, crouched in shadow, like a danger ready to burst out and take us away. For some of us, this disillusion process is never-ending. A whole life may sometimes not be enough to work this illusion through, to accept that we will not be able to grasp everything, manage anything, embrace everything, do anything, to accept the limitations of time, of space ... starting with one's own limitations. Sometimes the illusion of omnipotence can go as far as inventing an "Other" self.

> I have been deeply affected by Man's oldest protean temptation: that of multiplicity. I had the perfect illusion of a new creation of myself, by myself. [...] I had dispossessed myself ... dream was present at my expense. [Romain Gary, quoted by Regine Robin in "Il existe une tendance a emprunter n'importe quelle identite" (there exists a tendency to borrow any kind of identity): *Liberation*, 20–21 April 2002]

The strong comeback of that illusion of omnipotence has been especially facilitated since the development of twentieth century technology—including its latest phase, the Internet, which speeds up the globalization process to the point, sometimes, of a fantasy of ubiquity.

> Technology gives us almost divine powers: omnipotence, ubiquity, speed of light, power over life and death, abolition between desire and reality. This latter power is diabolical. God can be perceived in Nature. In other words in the malediction of being human. Of being condemned to being able to imagine what we cannot reach. To being able to wonder about being gods, but not actually being gods. [Marco-Antonio de la Parra (1999), *Open letter to Pinochet*, Le Serpent a Plumes, Paris, 1999]

Any system can be the victim of these illusions of power, be it in relation to itself or in relation to other systems or sub-systems. Here are two examples.

> The abuse of position at the top, of which big American corporations like Microsoft or Intel, or, more recently, European ones like Schneider Electric are often accused, are examples of the effects that an illusion of omnipotence can produce on the whole business system. How could their leaders ignore the threat that the laws in favour of competition represented for their company, if not by the fact of a blind fascination towards power? The very hierarchical configuration of some companies within the energy sector, or the services sector, is probably linked to the position of monopoly that they have often enjoyed over a long period of time, as well as to the nature of their product. The position of monopoly that the State had granted these companies had given them an imposing power that their leaders, as if by mimesis, have ended up implementing within their very organizations at times of (re)structuring.Very close to the illusion of omnipotence, from which it is derived, we have the one of omniscience, which tends towards the feeling of *omnipresence* (ubiquity). He who lives in this illusion thinks about the world by adding it up to what he can apprehend. He feels himself to be everywhere at once, just like other people (or himself) might think themselves able of managing anything, or knowing everything. We can see here one of the essential characteristics of totalitarianism.

> There is mention here of a god who is so infinite, so omnipresent that he has to give up a part of himself in order to create. He therefore accepts to give himself limits in order to generate the universe,

leaving within it a minute part of his divine light: ten tiny emana-
tions held in ten vases, called the ten "sephiroth". [Pietro Citati,
referring to the cosmogony developed in the sixteenth century by
the Jewish cabbalist Isaac Louria, in "We need myths to remain
humans": interview by Fabienne Pascaud for *Telerama 2561*, 10
February 1999]

Thus, the illusion of omnipresence consists in applying to space
what the illusion of immortality represents in time.

Immortality

> what a selfish idea people have of wanting to live forever . . . as if
> they wanted the Earth only for themselves, and for no one else.
> [Joyce Carol Oates (1995), *Confessions from a Gang of Girls*, Stock]

> . . . death came into my life at the age when one still believes his
> parents to be immortal. [Jacques Marette, embalmer: *Liberation*, 11
> January 200]

> . . . with, all of a sudden, a great discovery about death, at roughly
> the age of eight. Something very clear. I was sitting down in front
> of a fire burning in the fireplace, in the little house that my parents
> owned in the countryside . . . I suddenly became aware of existence,
> and its finitude, a kind of vertigo of existing. That I had to do some-
> thing. [Gerard Jugnot, actor: *Liberation*, 16 April 2001]

The discovery of the finite characteristic of our life makes us come
out of the illusion of immortality. Death seems to be an alien
concept for a child. He might discover it at times through experience when a close relative dies. Why this illusion? Perhaps simply
because children—in a similar way, on that issue, to institutions—
are made to satisfy their parents' desire of projecting themselves
into the future in spite of the ephemeral aspect of their life. To put
it another way, to have children is to respond to a desire to prolong,
not our own life, but the imprint that each of us leaves in this world.
But isn't there a risk, then, of projecting this illusion of immortality
on to our children? This could be the origin of their disillusion at
around the age of six, when they become aware of the fact that their
parents are not immortal. In any case, this disillusion is never
neutral. Understanding and accepting that life is time-limited

pushes each of us to give it a meaning, first of all through action and through taking initiatives. It invites us to create and achieve by ourselves by questioning the dependency process that surrounds us and hinders us.

Omniscience

> I do not know what. And not, please note: I know nothing, purely and simply, without specifying or distinguishing. I don't know nothing at all, nor am I saying that there is nothing. [. . .] Nescio "quid": what this rhetorical form is, I do not know; but there is something that I do not want to or cannot say, and to which I am directly referring when I use this negative form. [Vladimir Jankelevitch, "The je-ne-sais-quoi and the almost nothing". English version's reference not known]

It is around adolescence that we discover that omniscience, too, is an illusion, when we learn that our parents' knowledge is limited. There, too, could it be that projection is a primary mechanism in the elaboration of this original illusion? As if the adolescent had to carry, projected on to him and accepted by him, the illusion that the student is there to surpass his master, at least to nourish and prolong his knowledge. Omniscience is the same illusion that leads us to believe that, even if not everything is known, if everything is not explained, everything is nevertheless knowable and explainable, that everything is perceivable, and that, once more, it is not useful to choose—and, by that very action, to give something up. In this illusion, the reliance on a unique system of thought prevents any kind of surprise: in that way, the ideology of Reason can be seen to have excluded any kind of work with the Unconscious. As for the dogma of pontifical infallibility, a Catholic expression of the illusion of omniscience, it seems regularly to find itself the ally of some of the most tenacious resistances to social transformations. To lose the illusion of omniscience, or rather to recognize it as such, pushes us truly towards learning; that is to say, to begin our learning from experience.[23] At times the IT tool, when it is garnished with this almost magical aura, is the springboard for this illusion of omniscience. Everything becomes repairable and quantifiable, everything can now be tested and checked. Hence the mushrooming of "indicators" which run through the company from end to end, creating a mathematical image of the institution while silencing any element that could jeopardize the perfection of this model.

The original illusion of completeness

> ... some of the greatest achievements of man, he owes them to the painful feeling of the incompleteness of his destiny. Mediocre minds are, generally, fairly satisfied with communal life; they smooth over, as a figure of speech, their existence and make up for what could still be missing by vanity's illusions; but the sublime in mind, feelings and actions owes its soaring to the need for escape from the confines that circumscribe the imagination. [Madame de Stael (1998), *De la littérature*, Paris: Classiques Garnier]

> ... anxiety comes up when there is lack of lacking. [Jacques Lacan]

> I could already see myself / LEAD role on this poster ... My name was spreading / THREE times bigger / THAN anyone else's ... [Charles Aznavour, *Je m'voyais deja*. Music and lyrics: C. Aznavour]

Life instinct/death instinct ... all/nothing ... desire/lack ... Eros/Thanatos ... omnipotence/immortality/omniscience ... The identification of these three major illusions makes it possible for us to suppose that there is, upstream, an even more fundamental illusion, which links them all with one another, transcends them, and gives them all their breadth. That illusion is one of completeness, true negation of lack, which imposes on to every being the need to recompose a lost unity, an indescribable fusion where everything is possible, where everything can be known, where nothing disappears. Then comes the initial trauma (which will probably condition any separation experienced from then on), that of the separation with the mother, both physical and psychic: expelling from the uterus, moving away of the arms, of the breast, of the mother's body. When we are born, this illusion marks each of us with a deep and archaic imprint: *the illusions' matrix, which becomes the shaping foundation for the three major illusions.* In other words, the illusion of the mother is the mother of illusions. If one is not ready to psychically differentiate from his/her own mother, he/she remains a prime target for all the illusions that cross him/her. On the contrary, to work on the illusion of an exclusive relation with one's mother facilitates the work of transformation of illusions: it makes this process of disillusionment more fruitful, creative, and efficient.

The temptation of looking for and sinking into this original illusion is great. However, boundaries that cannot be bypassed do erupt and request from us that we put this illusion into perspective: the absence of the mother, the finitude of life and the vacuum created by death, the impossibility of apprehending everything (beings or objects), the limited aspect of our mind, so many manifestations of this lack that invite us to pass beyond this impasse. The original illusion of completeness thus invites us to find, in the face of lack, an immediate response—envy,[24] first of all—as a way of covering, filling in, negating this lack. However, by doing this, it denies to us access to something that lack generates in us that is most powerful: desire.[25] From that perspective, envy is truly death of desire, the latter being encountered only through accepting incompleteness and lack. Let us make a link also between the original illusion of completeness and the fourth Basic Assumption in Group Relations held dear by Pierre Turquet.[26] This Basic Assumption, called "Oneness" (Ba Oneness, or BaO), attributes the loss of identity and the weakening of differentiating processes witnessed in large systems to the fantasy that leads some of the system's members to confuse their own identity with that of the group, in other words to identify themselves with the institution itself, as if accepting to be only a small, insignificant part of the whole sets into motion the illusion of completeness.[27] Thus, the first moments of our life give us the opportunity of going beyond this powerful illusion of completeness; opportunity that we take more or less readily, depending on the circumstances. Having said that, the imprint that this illusion has forged in us remains deep, more or less active for the rest of our life. It also makes up the structure within which the three major illusions will successively be born, develop in order to be themselves, and, when the time comes, overcome. To accept one's humanity and one's humility (both share the same etymologic root, that of *humus*[28]), is to become an adult. This transformation is probably closely linked to the moving through the four intricate and successive processes of disillusion (see Figure 1). It is also to meet the opportunities offered by each of these processes: the acquisition of language, the invitation to action, the beginning of learning from experience. Did religions not indeed recognize this

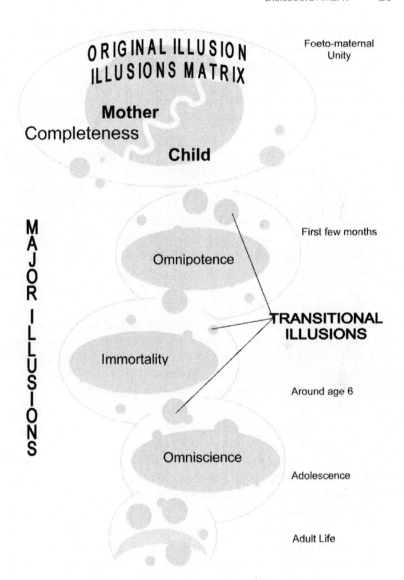

Figure 1. Matrix of original illusions.

intimate schedule in child development when they institutionalized rites of passage at the very moment of the major illusions' coming up to awareness? For example, for Jews, boy circumcision at birth, *bat mitzvah* for girls aged twelve, *bar mitzvah* for boys aged thirteen;

or again for Catholics, with baptism at birth, first communion at around age nine, profession of faith around age twelve, and, later on, confirmation. Finally, let us note that when grappling with each of these four illusions, the child faces one of the real or symbolic figures within his family. Indeed he constructs the original illusion of completeness in his dialogue with his mother. As for the three major illusions, it is again with his mother that he discovers the illusion of omnipotence, but also with his father when the latter comes and cuts through the mother–child relationship in its most fusional aspect. Immortality also concerns both parents. Finally, in his working through omniscience, the child turns towards his father (real or symbolic) who is supposed to understand everything and know everything. As for the combination of these four illusions, it would seem to refer directly to the representation that man has of God, all at once unique, almighty, immortal, and omniscient.

> Religious doctrines are all illusions, they cannot be proved and no one can be forced into holding them for truths, into believing in them. The desire that they realise is one of being protected and loved by a father more powerful than the real father. [Sophie de Mijolla-Mejor (2002), quoting Sigmund Freud (*The Future of an Illusion*, 1927) in *Dictionnaire International de la Psychanalyse*, p. 790, Paris: Calmann-Levy]

Transitional illusions

Transitional, rather than residual. The breathing movement of illusion–disillusion! is a living process that lasts throughout our existence. Illusions come and go, one after the other, one generating another by its very disappearance. They combine with one another and bind with each other, but in each case, they have an essential role in the development and the transformation of every individual. They contribute to our maturing. They make possible the temporary containment of anxiety that the passing through or beyond each milestone generates. It is because they play this essential role in the various transitions in our life that we call them in that way. Transitional illusions form and develop on the debris (or the imprints) left over by the four illusions already mentioned. In order to generate them, several processes are possible.

Combining illusions

In the first instance, the combining of the original and major illusions. Let us look at a few examples. We can at times get obsessed by a man's or a woman's *beauty*. It is, however, an illusion that mobilizes, for the one who experiences it, his/her representation of the ageing process and the illusion of being able to control it. Thus, the illusion of beauty can be interpreted as relying on the combining of the illusions of immortality and omnipotence. The illusion of *permanence* is at play as much within individuals as it is within human organizations.

> Everything must change so that nothing will change. [Tomasi de Lampedusall Gattopardo, English version's reference not known]

It involves the principle of homeostasis applied to both individual and collective systems: both have, by nature, a "co-substantial" tendency to maintain the state within which they exist, a tendency that vehemently opposes any attempt at transformation. Thus, this illusion implies considering human organizations as caught up in an ineluctable constancy that renders any modification or improvement impossible. This illusion has its roots both in the original illusion of completeness—as seen in the lack of desire—and in the major illusions of omnipotence and immortality. *Individualism* is a more and more frequently observed human behaviour that is founded on the idea of self-sufficiency and autarchy. Undoubtly it is linked to the major illusions of omnipotence and omniscience, themselves in direct connection with the original illusion of completeness. The disillusion process that it can generate leads to the discovery of one dimension of human condition: beginning to recognize the other, understanding the necessity to connect with him. *Possessing objects*, enjoying material wealth, are for a large part an illusion linked to the illusion of immortality: we are only passing through, while objects, such as diamonds, have a much greater life span than we do. For the collector, this illusion appears to be also linked to an illusion of omnipotence (of owning everything), even maybe of omniscience. Indeed, how could we not mention *castration*, symbolic representation of the threat of the phallus's disappearance, which the illusion of completeness directly calls upon: according to Freud, the castration complex leads the little boy to deny any difference between sexes; whereas for Lacan, the subject only exists through castration, which rearticulates lack and makes it possible to exist, thanks to this loss.

> It is the Assumption of castration which creates lack onto which desire is founded. Desire reproduces the subject's relationship to the object. [Jacques Lacan, *Writings*]

More generally, the illusion of completeness invites us to link castration anxiety to a reduction, an amputation, a weakening, a loss of power that cannot be exceeded. However, accepting castration—or bereavement (see above)—can also help us to understand that castration is nothing other than an incompleteness that unveils very directly our lack, our desire for action; given also that it pushes us towards an encounter with the Other, the absent member, with a view to forging an interaction that will fertilize the differences that it draws together.

> One of our partners, a public sector company in the Anglo-Saxon world, is hesitant in the face of a "painful" decision: drastically cutting down staffing levels despite an obviously unfavourable political climate (close to election time). Our attention focused on the verb used to refer to this reduction: "cutting down" . . . If the institution, starting with its leaders, sees this reduction in staffing as a castration within a context of an illusion of completeness, then it will sink into the state that we see it in: loss of power, stagnation, inability to decide, to act, and to transform. That is forgetting that castration, when you move beyond this illusion of completeness, can lead to the opposite: the institutional encounter with lack as the source of a resurgence in desire that makes it possible for it to construct a true becoming.

Counter-illusions

The formation of transitional illusions does not result solely from the combining of more fundamental illusions. They are sometimes produced by the negation of the latter ones, for which they become an opposite illusion, a *counter-illusion*. For example, the saviour is a role that one encounters often in institutions. According to us, it is the result of a systemic construction, a lot more collective and interactive than it is individual. The example called *perfection* (*a god amongst men*) referred to earlier is a fairly good account of what the role of saviour can entail. Thus, on the one hand the saviour seems caught into an illusion of omnipotence. But he could not take up that role without the—at least passive—complaisance of those around him. Those are caught into the counter-illusion to omnipotence: *the illusion of impotence*. To make explicit the way in which these crossing illusions are at play makes it possible to formulate, at least roughly, a possible understanding of the totalitarian processes at work in dictatorships or in sects.The illusion of impotence is one by which the individual thinks of himself as a "poor little thing" unfit for action, capable at best of being mothered, lost in a world for which he doesn't count, dependent exclusively on others and not on himself. Perhaps this illusion finds its origin in the refusal to accept the rupture of the umbilical cord and the loss of the mother's breast. Hence the success of this new type of phone, so accurately called "mobile" or "cellular", a new kind of technological—and oh so logical—umbilical cord! The temptation is great to allow oneself to be swept by events, without making any decisions, without choosing, a puppet swaying to the good will of others—who are then projected into a role of almighty. Any inclination for action then appears useless, and dies as soon as it appears: we cannot do anything about it, we will never be able to change anything, the situation is too strong. Everything seems complicated, impossible, useless. Only desire makes it possible to come out of this illusion and to become aware of one's own authority (that is to say, following its etymology, *of one's own capacity to be the author of one's actions*). Another illusion sometimes is to believe that what we are doing has no importance whatsoever. This *illusion of futility*,[29] the counter-illusion of immortality, leads to the belief that the action that I am undertaking now has no impact either on the system as it is existing now, nor on the system as it will exist, and that only nothingness can respond to my existence. At the personal level, though not exclusively, this triggers behaviours of self-negation, atony, apathy, carelessness, which can go as far as depression and self-destruction. If we are mortal, if everything is mortal and nothing depends on us, then we might as well do nothing. The fear of death then makes us scared of living, of engaging in projects without knowing in advance what their outcome will be.

Generously offer yourself to life . . . [Giorgio Strehler]

But institutions, as systems, are not sheltered from that illusion. Behind the ideology of an inexhaustible world and of limitless material progress, isn't there also this same fantasy that after all, mortality being the absolute queen, it is useless to think about what can follow, or about whom might outlive us?

We can reflect, as an example, on the contradiction that exists within many public or private sector companies for which the ecological impact on their environment is significant, even possibly irreversible. These companies, whose mental representation is built on a "speerian" model (*an empire for a thousand years*), who offer their members status "for life", appear to be wanting to ignore the implications that their products have on the biological world, the long-term implications of their decisions then running the risk of being under-estimated. In other words, the quality of what they produce contradicts the perenniality that they appear to seek. Could the illusion of immortality and the illusion of futility be unconsciously combining? Equally, we can talk about the *illusion of ignorance* as a mirror to the one of omniscience. It is not only about the collusion or complacency processes by which an individual or a system hides the truth and *does not want to know*, but also about the illusion of not understanding anything, illusion according to which reality reveals itself to be impossible to perceive clearly and distinctly, and where the opacity of things renders them intangible. The complexity of institutions, their watertight compartmentalizing, the speed at which actions must be achieved, feed this illusion: the flow of information submerges anyone who would want to pay attention to the knowledge of things, and the impossibility of working your way up to the very source of information dries up the search for its primary causes. To entertain the illusion of not knowing is to take pleasure in a vacuum of meaning. It is striking oneself of vacuity, it is closing the door on any possibility for surprises. *When it comes to Eros, the counter-illusion could be one of suffering,* which opposes pleasure and leads, perhaps, to sado-masochism. *With Thanatos, the original counter-illusion,* founder of all counter-illusions, a kind of wild or archaic reaction in the face of desire *is one of inanity,*[30] complete occultation of desire, by which we do not want to estimate what we are capable of, what we know, what we are. They are flights, acting-outs that refuse the "act of passage".[31] The faith in another world that would come and justify this one may come from this self-denial.[32] Remaining in an illusion of a somewhere else and of a "later on" enables us to not own up to desire in what it has that is most deeply subversive, to not take up our own authority through projecting anything that could happen on the initiative of others rather than our own (with, as corollary, the illusion that they will do it for me, and that they will do it better). The plenitude of joy, the ecstatic experience, the capacity to experiment and to learn, the encounter with the Other, are many open doors to desire. To recognize, along one's journey, that we are the fruit of a desire (whatever it may be, conscious or unconscious) and that we are an object of desire makes it possible also to consider ourselves as worthy of meaning, and capable of being the subject of (or subjected to) desire. Let us say it once more, *in no instance are illusions either good or bad; they are always useful in their genesis.* They are simply constitutive of the human condition. In the era of self-development and self-transformation, they offer the possibility for transitions, for milestones; at least only when the awareness—more or less lengthy and late—of what each of them can generate afterwards does not come either too soon, or too late! Illusions inhabit us, we use them at times as safe havens, at other times as springboards that help us reach new milestones, at other times still as compensation processes that put up a wall between us and what we only accept to look at with great reluctance: our imperfection, our incompleteness, our lack, but also our capacity, our authority, our desire. It is in that way that they can keep us in the background of our own life. As for life's journey, is it not about revealing them, and then transforming them through a disillusion process?

A bulwark to vertigo

We are suggesting here that the acceptance of reality is an endless task and that no human being manages to free himself from the tension created by the relationship between internal and external reality; we are also suggesting that this tension can be relieved by the existence of an intermediate area of experience which is not contested (arts, religion, . . .). This intermediate area is in direct continuation with the play area of the small child 'lost' in his game. [D. W. Winnicott (1953), *Transitional Objects and Transitional Phenomena, A Study of the First Not-me Possession.*

> It is sheer madness to hope to understand anything in this
> world without having previously received some kind of an idea,
> however vague it may be. Before attempting to get rid of our
> assumptions, we must first of all take them seriously. It is only then
> that we have the duty of forming a better judgement. [. . .] "under-
> standing" always means "understanding differently". [Hans-Georg
> Gadamer]

By mobilizing our personal and institutional experiences, we have
so far identified, in the form of hypotheses, the range and system
of illusions that each of us will come across. We can see, though,
that these illusions have a very clear function: they are the parapet
(in French, *garde-fou*, meaning literally protection for/from the
mad) of our existences and of its corollary anxiety at the time when
we are confronting reality and becoming aware of how vast the
world actually is and how tragic our lives can be. By allowing us to
"buy" a bit of time, each illusion protects us from a vertigo that
would be unbearable, that would drive us mad. By implicitly
supposing until the age of six that he is immortal, the child prepares
himself for the discovery of the reality of death when the time is
right, in other words when his psychic constitution allows him to
bear it without excessive panic that could lead to a breakdown.
Being in an illusion of continuity with his mother's body allows
him to withstand the trauma of birth before pursuing the slow
process of autonomy and emancipation that will lead him to adult-
hood. Believing oneself to be omniscient enables the escape from
the vertigo of this frantic production of knowledge that no one
these days is truly capable of grasping. Being in an illusion of
omnipotence makes it possible to apprehend the universe, with its
unthinkable limits, with temporarily lesser risk. Illusions are as
many temporary protections against anxiety. Protections more than
defences in that their role seems to be to contain anxiety so as to
protect an adequate space for a person's growth.[33] Having said that,
as with any protection, its crucial effect is in the quality of the
process that will lead to its own overcoming. Temporarily, it enables
growth. Maintained for too long, it stops any exposition of that
individual to reality, to its environment, and to others: it then
becomes counter-productive, antagonistic to this growth and this
transformation.

3. Disillusionment

Because we are destroying illusions, we are being accused of jeopardising ideals. [Sigmund Freud (1910), "Future chances for analytic therapy"]

CLOWN, bringing down in mockery, in the grotesque, in roaring laughter, the meaning that against all light I had made of my importance.

I will dive.

Pouchless into the underlying infinite-spirit open to everyone,
Myself open to a new and incredible dew
By dint of being worthless And blank . . . And laughable . . ." [Henri Michaux (1939), "The space within Clown": in *Peintures*, Paris, Gallimard]

The disillusionment process

The disillusionment process—which leads to the state of disillusion[34]—is one that makes it possible for us to stop being the victim of an illusion (including and especially with our own complaisance), to take ourselves out of it, out of its hold on us. After a while, it renews our link with reality by allowing us to invest ourselves more fully in it, with our own desire and our own lack— laid bare or, at least, clarified in parts in that experience—rather than to continue to distort it.

As process, disillusionment works through time and can be analysed in terms of transformation. To say that means perceiving this process as uncertain, irregular, more or less chaotic, slaloming amongst resistances and consequently marked by the alternating of progressions and regressions, of constructions and destructions, or even deconstructions, and touching on something very deep, the very essence of a being (individual or collective) and of his psychic life (see Figure 2). The major illusions, and upstream the original illusion of completeness, surface one after the other, at times in people's life that are probably similar from one individual to another. Each illusion goes through a more or less lengthy phase of impregnation, through a varyingly slow maturing which leads to the emergence of awareness. The acknowledgement of the latter

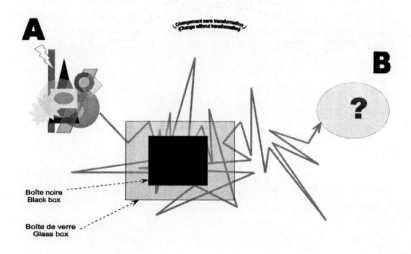

Figure 2.   Transformation.

triggers the disillusionment process. The refusal of this awareness, conversely, leads to the reinforcement of this illusion, to take pleasure in it as part of an entropic and mortifying repetition process which, indeed, does not exclude some kind of enjoyment. Perhaps this kind of refusal surfaces when maturing has not taken place, when a major illusion happens too early or too late, too slightly or too strongly. Or perhaps when its role as defence against anxiety overwhelms the individual and over-controls him, at the cost of a dependence that renders him incapable of overcoming it or transforming it.

A four-stage process

Nevertheless, the disillusionment process has four successive and intertwined phases.[35] Let us take the example of the illusion of immortality as a way of describing them. The first phase is that of *unawareness*. At that stage death is not an issue, since the child does not yet know that his life is limited. He then discovers, around the age of six, the existence of death. This *awareness* leads (or at least can lead) to a double movement. Whereas rationality recognizes this discovery and tries to accommodate it, underneath much more violent movements are at play: powerful defence mechanisms are put into action to deny this discovery, obscure its consequences, and bury the awareness. It is then the passage into the *unconscious*, in other words the third phase, which, for many of us, is the last one: the ambivalence that we entertain with our condition as mortal being comprises a conscious, rational, more or less referred to and accepted level; and an unconscious level that is no other than the illusion of immortality of which we now know the consequences by the way in which each of us engages with his existence. Following this we can argue that *disillusionment* is the process by which some of us decide to fight against these mechanisms of occultation, of displacement, of repression, and this in order to extract our condition of mortal being from its unconscious state, to inscribe it explicitly in our psyche, and to translate it in a concrete way through an appropriate transformation of our behaviour. It then becomes obvious that it is only when the disillusionment process has started that we can, progressively, appreciate that we were dealing with an illusion. Thus, what the child ignores through a simple lack of awareness is forcefully occulted by the adult into the unconscious. Having said that, to be *truly* adult, isn't that being constantly confronted by this process of illusions–disillusionment? Everyone, of course, engages on a unique journey that is his/her own. But generally, these four phases greatly overlap within the same learning process that becomes even more progressive when each stage feeds another. Similarly, the major illusions follow one another. Thus, no stage can be bypassed. For example, to grapple with the illusion of omniscience necessitates that one has clearly started his work of disillusion of immortality.

Resistances

> Is future a given, as seem to suggest Newton's laws, or is the universe in perpetual construction? [Ilya Prigogine (1996) "The end of certainties: time, chaos and the laws of nature", *Coll. Opus*, Odile Jacob, Paris.

> I would go to the end of the earth, / I would dye my hair blond / If you asked me to . . . [Edith Piaf, *La vie en rose*. Lyrics: Edith Piaf; music: Louigy, 1942]

True transformation is presented by the disillusionment process as the passage from one mode of response to life and death drives to another. In the example of personal mourning, the process at work is one of "eye opening": if the person that I loved has died, then the whole world can die. This powerfully obvious statement, always previously known but always avoided, suddenly appears in all its clarity, and shines a different light on the meaning that I can give to my life in the here-and-now. An illusion is therefore one possible response to incompleteness. It involves a distortion of reality that kindly spares us an examination of our imperfection as well as of our authority. Becoming aware of this mechanism enables us to embark on a real process of transformation of that illusion towards a different response to lack, one of desire. In passing, the misleading characteristic of the distortion is exposed and replaced by a true investment in a dialectic, complementary, and interactive relationship between lack and desire. Consequently, the acknowledgment of both desire and lack triggers in turn other transformations, this time in what makes up our daily life.

> He is happily disillusioned . . . [Michel Polac (referring to Jean Baudrillard) *Liberation*, 5 February 2000]

This process is sometimes marked, at the beginning, by a revelation, a flash of insight, a lightning. But it cannot be reduced solely to that. The passage is neither regular, nor continuous: it hits irregular resistances, and the movement of transformation then adopts a trajectory made of zigzags, of progressions and regressions, of constructions and deconstructions (see above), which are many clues confirming the authenticity of a transformation process.[36] *If disillusionment is a process that the transformation approach describes easily, it may be because it represents its best example, maybe even its core principle.* The journey through which we "lose" our illusions (original, major, transitional) constitutes a series of stages through which a human being, in order to become Man and to live, rids himself of his various illusions one after the other—not without any regression, not without giving them up totally or for good, not without generating at least temporarily, and along the way, transitional illusions. Let us take an example.

At SNCF (French Railways), the illusion for the social body is a very strong tendency to idealize its President. Thus, Michel Fournier was seen as a god. Arriving at the head of the company, Jean Bergougnoux is also idealized, but rather like a saviour, given the considerable difficulties facing the company. He attempts to foil this plot of idealization, as indicated by a key-phrase in his speech: take your own destiny in your own hands! Sadly, without any success. From saviour, he becomes persecutor, then victim, and comes close to being ejected from the system. Having understood the situation, he wants to intervene, but he does not have the time or the capacity to go beyond the speech. Given the resistances at work in the institution and the external political decisions, he will not be able to overcome this situation, which leads to the November–December 1995 strikes. Conscious of the work of his predecessor, Loik Le Floch-Prigent also follows his analysis and his avenues for action. But his method is more direct. The new president for SNCF knows that a sword of Damocles is hanging above his head (the politico–legal imbroglio of the ELF affair). He therefore attempts to move things on as quickly as possible, knowing that he can be pushed aside at any time. His imprisonment happens in early July 1996. Handcuffed, dragged through the mud, jailed, publicly confronted with his possible weaknesses and past mistakes, he nevertheless enables the company's social body to question the idealization process that it had been feeding on: can gods really be shown handcuffed for all to see? For the paradox is that he has been both a very good president for SNCF—but also for Gaz de France where he has left a very strong memory—and that he shows how human he is; that is to say, neither an untouchable nor a saint. Consequently, nothing is like it was before at SNCF. Once the presidential status has been repatriated from Mount Olympus to the bosom of the human condition, the new president can act with a much greater margin for manoeuvre than the one he would have known without the apparent failure of his two predecessors. For now that he is perceived as a man—and not as a god or as a devil—he is also now considered as mortal. And, following from that, so is the company. It then becomes absolutely crucial that every stakeholder within the company takes up their role. And, at the same time, their destiny in their own hands.

Here, disillusionment operates through stages. Very strong resistances lead to very violent regressions (strikes in December 1995, departure of Le Floch-Prigent in July 1996 . . .) which have the potential of generating serious questioning leading to progressions, providing, though, that the leaders have the courage to engage with it. This example shines light on the nature of the disillusionment process, which constitutes, in its institutional dimension, a true transformation. A transformation that makes other transformations possible. Disillusion here goes through intermediate stages during which certain roles—Bergougnoux, Le Floch-Prigent as Presidents—act as transitional objects: they provide support for a disillusionment process while continuing to feed a part of the illusion. Thus, as for the individual, a system cannot come out all at once from its illusions. It goes through intermediate illusions that allow the zigzagging journey towards the temporary outcome of the disillusion process: the (always partial) leaving behind of illusions.

Building one's freedom

Lucidity is the injury that is closest to the sun. [Rene Char]

The forbidden fruit

To "live" in illusion (or, more precisely, among illusions), to be satisfied with the protection that they provide, is like existing without facing oneself or others. It is refusing the dereliction of the human condition in order to seek refuge in a somewhere else, whether it is heaven or hell; it is refusing, in the same token, the transcendence inherent to this condition by hiding it behind veils. The illusion is to believe that life is as we would like it to be, to distort reality to the point of accommodating to it by denying the obvious. We then become prisoner of an escape route in which, given the range of self, cultural, or social inhibitions, we do not allow ourselves *to bite into the Forbidden Fruit*. In other words, to embody the real, to open up to knowing it, to impact on the course of things, to modify their meaning by our very existence, to taste life. Thus, to hold back, or deny our desire—or to give it complete and utter priority (which results in the same!)—rather than to engage it lucidly leads to preferring immediate and transitory satisfactions, to which we soon become accustomed. Like a soft drug, or even a hard one, we are tempted to renew its use more and more frequently because it brings about an ephemeral and repeated pleasure, and this despite the guilt that this experience also generates. In a Judeo-Christian perspective, the primary question remains confined to a binary alternative ("Am I or am I not omnipotent, or omniscient, or even eternal, or complete . . .?") which reinforces repetition and confines it to illusion. Strangled by Thanatos or stunned by Eros, asphyxiated by anxiety or overwhelmed by enjoyment, the individual denies the complexity of the link between life and death. He prefers to build around himself a refuge that is seemingly comfortable and protective yet disconnected, at least in part, from the reality that surrounds it. Other kinds of self-questioning are then pushed to the background, into the shadow: these are the ones that would trigger a true disillusionment, indeed bringing about an awareness and the giving up of past certainties, but at the high cost of painful feelings.

The Promised Land

So then the ubiquitous salesman said to the farmer, "Can you put me up for the night?' Whereupon the farmer said, "Sure, but you'll have to sleep with my son." "Good Lord," said the salesman, "I'm in the wrong joke." [Richard Prince (1989) "The salesman and the farmer", in *Agenda Autrement*, Paris]

Reaching the Promised Land is an illusion, too: the Promised Land in reality is never reached (and not only for Moses). For each of us, it keeps moving as we engage in our own progression, renewing constantly the gap, the void that separates us from it and that feeds, again and again, our energy, our libido, our desire. This exodus is also a metaphor that speaks about an internal journey,[37] about the encounter with this self who is at the same time an other to be discovered step by step. This journey is one of disillusionment. This exodus is one of coming out of the golden (or black) cage of illusions and of the protection that they claim to generate. It requires that we give ourselves the authority to engage in it, to travel on it. It does not lead to perfection, but to the joy of true self-construction and self-actualization. Crucially, it makes it possible to experience and recognize lack (in French, *connaitre et reconnaitre*). When the disillusionment process goes far enough—indeed crossing the powerful affects characteristic of all transformation processes including phases of depression—it allows the construction, bit by bit, of one's own relative freedom. Freedom, here, is to be understood as awareness, for it is the capacity to apprehend directly, without sidetracking, the dialectic play between emptiness and full-ness, desire and lack. Thus, resistances to disillusionment are likely to originate in fright (in French *effroi*[38]) generated by episodes of depression unavoidable in this transformation process. To depression, we all too often prefer either a state of daily, ordinary, bland survival, or an experience of hectic, excited, and intoxicating hyper-life. The disillusionment process is similar to Occam's razor, whose refutations lead this English theologian to get rid of a whole cohort of under-divinities (seraphs, cherubs, . . .) that tradition and super-stition had allowed to proliferate in Christian religion. Disillusionment is that constant process that helps us to live in the here and now by giving body and desire to our projects and our activities, by making us closer to our condition of in-between, between Eros and Thanatos. To live instead of being in the state of survival in a daily triviality that means that every day cannot but look like the previous one, in a likely attempt to abolish time that passes us by and put back the ineluctable deadline. Survival could be the result of counter-illusions (impotence, ignorance, futility): in a vacuum of meaning, the only possible behaviour becomes repeti-tion, the negation of surprises brought about by desire. The direct application of the illusions of omnipotence, omniscience, and immortality, however, could very well be what we call hyperlife (in French *frenevie*): a mix of frenzy, hysteria, burning out, hyperlife consumes individual lives for the benefit—in the short term—of the institution's success, but most often does not allow the construction of a solid and perennial institution. To bite into the Forbidden Fruit, the one of knowledge, makes it paradoxically possible to recognize the ineluctable limits of one's own knowledge! Then can appear, supremely, the ardent obligation to the Other, to one's relationship to the other, to others. Thus, learning and containment will be facil-itated and expanded in the face of the indispensable processes of disillusionment. To aspire to the Promised Land, the one of completeness, makes it paradoxically possible to recognize that it will never be reached! Then can rise, serenely, the discovery that the promised land resides in the journey and not in the destination, in pulsation and not in stillness, in the here and now and not in the there and then. It is in the dialectic between desire and lack that the disillusionment process is created. Conversely, the original illusion persists when we do not believe in both any more, but in only one of these two poles, or, even better, when we do not want to allow ourselves to be touched by the other pole any more. Working through one's own freedom, constructing and engaging on one's own journey, means losing the illusion that the journey has already been planned out by oneself or by others. It means losing the illusion that everything is possible all at once. It means accepting the travel, the passage from one state to another, from one form to another, from birth to death . . . for any system. It means accepting transformation in what it holds that is most surprising and unintentional, the not-planned. It means giving ourselves the authority to examine what we thought inexplorable and inexorable, in order to find in this to-and-fro between ideal and reality one's own truth, one's own relative freedom. Aren't illusions and disillusions, however indispensable both might be, through their dialectic interactions the sources of our humanity in its spiritual dimension, of democracy in its political dimension, of our interdependence in its psychic dimension? This text, between forbidden fruit and promised land, therefore has the sole ambition to inquire, again and again, into our human condition, incomplete, always becoming, always seeking, and, in a word, always transforming.

> It is the face of the wandering man, who does everything, knows everything, touches on everything, grasps everything, but who nevertheless still lives in the perpetual anxiety of having missed the essential bit and neglected the greatest. [Theodor Lessing (1930) *Self hatred*. Berlin, 1930: Berg international editeurs, Paris, 2001]

Notes

1. Here is a possible definition of system-in-the-mind (SIM). SIM is the systemic construction—the system—through which every individual represents, in an unconscious way if it is not worked through, his environment. This construction at least influences—but often determines—his relationships, his behaviour, his decisions, his vision of himself and his place in the universe. SIM comes directly from the person's history and his relationships with his original institutions (family, school, etc.). It structures the individual and conditions his relationships with institutions in the here and now.

2. As Daniel Sibony writes about May 1968: "The saddest of all are those who did not make any illusions there, sadder than those who lost theirs, or those who stayed there". In *Liberation*, 5 April 2001.

3. The etymological perspectives referred to in this article are borrowed from the *Dictionnaire historique de la langue francaise* directed by Alain Rey, editions Le Robert, Paris, 1998.

4. *¡Que ilusion ir esta noche al teatro!* What a joy to be going to the theatre tonight!

5. Meron Benvenisti's analysis of the Israeli-Palestinian issue and of the myths that it generates gives a good example of the way in which modern myths may be working:

> [. . .] like all myths [in the service of a cause], once it has caught on, it becomes more real than reality itself. Israeli society needs the myth, because it is unifying and justifies all actions, clears the conscience, defines the enemy as bloodthirsty and allows society to cope with the tough reality of "no alternative". [. . .] Myths are no illusions but a salad of real and legendary events aimed at creating an image that the society wants to show to the world and itself. [. . .] the trouble, of course, is that myths are inherently subjective for the society that creates them for its own needs, and that society's opponents create their own, contradictory myths, like mirror images [. . .] In such a binary situation, there is no place for a third party. If you don't buy the myth, you're against me, so I'll have to hire a better public relations firm to successfully sell you my self-image. [. . .] if we stick to the myth, we'll only continue to the march of folly. [Meron Benvenisti, "Challenging the Camp David myth", in *Ha'aretz*, 2 August 2001]

6. See the concept of "Free Trade Faith" developed by P. Bourdieu in his article "The essence of neo-liberalism", in *Le Monde Diplomatique*, March 1998, p. 3.

7. It is worth noting that in Spanish *"vega"* means "fertile valley, cultivated plain".

8. This article was first written in 1999. Since then, events have demonstrated the ravages of this illusion to which just about everybody had subscribed.

9. In French, *resver* (1130) and then *rever* (seventeenth century) are of an uncertain and unverifiable origin. According to some, they come from *esver*, meaning wandering, from the popular Latin *exvagus*, meaning wanderer. For others, they come from *raver*, meaning to be delirious,

in fury, raving, coming from the Latin words *rabere*, meaning raging and re-*exvadere*, meaning escaping from reality into imagination.

10. Borrowed from the Imperial Latin *fantasma*, meaning ghost, spectre, in low Latin image, representation through imagination, transcription of the Greek *phantasma*, meaning apparition, vision, ghost, from the same family as *pharein*, meaning to appear. The spelling *phantasy* is also in use, but the attempt at distinguishing both meanings depending on their spelling, in psychoanalysis, has failed. *Fantasy* means ghost in the fourteenth century, hallucinatory image in 1832 (a medical term), production of the image that enables the ego to escape reality according to Amiel in 1866, before the development of psychoanalysis.

11. Definition: representative activity, more or less creative, the contents of which are determined by sudden ideas and by weakened or modified memories of objects, events, and situations, including in their emotional meaning. (. . .) In that way, a product of imagination is different from hallucination by its complexity and its relationship to past sensory experiences. W. D. Frollich (1997), *Dictionnaire de la Psychologie, Collection Encyclopedies d'Aujourd'hui*, Paris: La Pochotheque, Le Livre de Poche.

12. Borrowed (1223) from the Imperial Latin *fictio*, meaning action of shaping, creation, and figuratively action of pretending and its result, a legal term in Low Latin and deceit in medieval Latin; *fictio* comes from *fictum*, supine of *fingere*, meaning to invent.

13. Telling stories, essential lies, in *Change International*, 3, 1985: 62.

14. Id.

15. In French, *leurres*, from a francisque *lothr*, meaning bait, in German *Luder*, this word is linked to the verb *lapon*, meaning to invite, of which several Germanic languages have a representative (*lapian* in old English, *laden* in German and medieval Dutch). With the general meaning of "that which attracts", the word has become specialized in falconry to mean, circa 1225, a piece of red leather in the shape of a bird decorated with feathers, used to bring the hunting bird back to the falconer's fist.

16. In French, *sidere*. If we look at the etymology of this word (to come under the fatal influence of stars, but also to be heat-struck) how can one not be amazed by the fact that the illusionist, just like the popular figure of a fairy, has a wand with a star on it? It is the fascination for the star that obscures our judgement, by throwing into darkness the magician's manipulations.

17. Arland Wrigley, in *Liberation*, 23 July 2001.

18. See D. Gutmann, R. Pierre, J. Ternier-David and C. Verrier (1999), "From envy to desire: witnessing the transformation", in *Group Relations, Management & Organization*, Oxford: Oxford University Press.
19. See brochures for Leading Consultation 2001–2002 and 2003–2004, a training programme for the role of consultant and the institutional transformation approach, organized by the International Forum for Social Innovation and the University of Glamorgan (Pontypridd, Wales, UK). The programme leads to a Diploma in Research, M.Phil, and Ph.D.
20. Let us quote on this issue Hannah Arendt, "Eichmann in Jerusalem, report on the banality of evil". English version not known.
21. The bulk of this text was written before 11 September 2001.
22. Melanie Klein, *Envy and Gratitude*. Details of English version not known.
23. See brochure for Leading Consultation referred to above.
24. Envy is an adaptation in the form of enveia (tenth century), then envy (1155), of the Classical Latin *invidia* (malevolence; jealousy; envy), from *invidus* (envious). This adjective comes from *invidere* (to look at with a malevolent eye) hence meaning harm and envying, made up of *in-* and *videre* which later on gave view. There is in *invidere* a link to the popular belief in the evil eye, for which the Indo-European character has been established; the use for hate has been made possible by the presence of other forms also meaning view, such as *specere*.
25. Desire comes from the phonetic reduction of the Latin term *desiderare* made up of *de-* (privative) and of *sideris* (the stars). Desire literally means to stop looking at the stars, in other words to acknowledge the absence of . . . with a strong nuance of regret.
26. Turquet, P. (1994), "Threats to identity", in L. Kreeger (Ed.), *The Large Group*.
27. We can also link it to the myth of lost completeness, in other words the search for fusion that gets generated by the passion of love, and that Eve illustrates when she is created out of Adam's rib. A lost completeness hiding another one? Based on Georges Zimra's statements, psychoanalyst in "The roads to knowledge, tropism in loving passion", Catherine Pont-Humbert, Doria Zenine, *France Culture*, 8 July 2002.
28. From the Latin *humus* (hearth, soil) which is linked to the Indo-European root *ghyom*, meaning hearth. Humble comes from *humilis*, meaning low, close to the earth, and, figuratively, modest, weak, conscious of his own weakness, which links directly to *humus*. Human

comes from *humanus*, meaning specific to man, cultured, civilized, benevolent, that can happen to a mortal man, linked to *homo, hominis*, itself derived from *humus*. Let us bear in mind that in Hebrew, Adam means the *glebean*, he who is made of *glebe* . . .

29. Futile, from the Latin *futilis*, meaning that which lets its content escape (when referring to a vase), hence, figuratively, deprived of depth, of seriousness. Linked to the Indo-European root *gheu-*, meaning letting run.

30. From *inanis*, meaning empty, vain, without any breath of life, itself deriving from the Indo-European root *ane*, meaning breath of life, which can be found also in *ame* (French for soul) or *anima*.

31. In French: passages *a l'acte* (acting-outs) *qui refusent "l'acte de passage"* from Marie Balmary (1995), *The Forbidden Sacrifice: Freud and the Bible*, Paris.

32. "Faith, everlasting sole for whoever stays still". Henri Michaux (1934), "Against!", in *La nuit remue*, Gallimard, Paris.

33. See Gutmann, D. (1989) *The Decline of Traditional Defences Against Anxiety. Proceedings of the First International Symposium on Group Relations*, F. Gabelnick & W. Carr, (Eds.), Keble College, Oxford, AK Rice Institute. (1990) "Le déclin des défenses traditionnelles contre l'anxiété". *Notes de Conjonctures Sociales* no. 342, Paris.

34. Note that both French and English have two words: Desillusion/disillusion (loss of an illusion) Desillusionment/disillusionment (act of getting somebody to lose their illusion; fact of being disillusioned, of feeling disillusioned).

35. See also Gutmann, D., Ternier-David, J., Verrier, C. (1996) Paradoxer och förvandling i konsultrollen : Från reparation till uppenbarelse (Paradoxe et transformation dans le rôle de consultant : de la réparation à la révélation). Den svårfångade organisationen, Stockholm.

36. See "Groupes et transformation", quoted above. See also Figure 2.

37. See Maurice Zundel (1986), *I is an Other*, Anne Sigier (Ed.).

38. *Effrayer* (to frighten): from the Latin *exfridare*, meaning to bring out of peace, of tranquility.

DIALOGUE OF LACKS

Dialogue of lacks

David Gutmann and Jean-François Millat*

I n every situation of crisis, such as relationships between states, between communities, between management and labour, or within a family or a couple, one can always find at least one actor or one observer to deplore the _lack of dialogue_ and to promote the establishment or re-establishment of a "real" dialogue between the parties.[1] Yet, we have to acknowledge that, even when the dialogue starts up, it very often aborts without generating the transformation of roles and systems seen as necessary to solve the crisis. What then is a "real" dialogue?

We intend here to argue the case for the following working hypothesis: the _lack of dialogue_ or its fruitlessness centres on the resistances and fear provoked by _dialogue of lacks_, which alone is able to authorize transformation and feed life.

This current reflection expands on a previous one published in the paper entitled "Disillusionment—from the Forbidden Fruit to

*With the contribution of members of PRAXIS INTERNATIONAL network
This English version has been established with the contribution of George Bruce
Irvine. It is the translation of a document in French entitled "Le dialogue des
manques".

the Promised Land" by David Gutmann, François-Michel van der Rest, Jacqueline Ternier-David and Christophe Verrier (2002).

For the stakeholders in a situation, be it a crisis or not, acknowledging the necessity of a dialogue between them implies each of them acknowledging and accepting that they alone are unable to propose a feasible way out of this situation; *starting up dialogue implies the acknowledgement and acceptance of one's incompleteness.*

The feeling of incompleteness is a matrix of illusions, feelings and behaviours informed by our human and social condition. Thus, it is the matrix of pain generated by lack within us and of joys generated by its satisfaction.[2] The way we live our incompleteness, the way we get in touch with it, determines our relationship to the other.

This feeling originates in the double, definitive and irreversible experience of each of us being separated from one's mother: physiological separation at birth and, later on, psychical separation when one has found himself or herself forbidden by the symbolic father to be "the mother's wholeness".

The separation from any loved one—by physical death or by breakdown of affective links—and mainly the separation from one's mother, revives these original experiences.

At birth, the child is not the only one having this experience; the mother has a symmetrical experience of separation and loss expressed by the "empty belly" feeling and post partum depression. The vital importance of this complete separation for the mother and the woman is demonstrated by the care taken by the obstetrician, after the arrival of the new-born child, to make sure the whole placenta—which belongs to the child—has been well delivered.

The trauma resulting from this double initial experience, and the anxiety that results from it, are bearable only by installing an illusionnement process: the illusion of being able to recompose a lost unity in an indescribable fusion, rather like a person who has a limb amputated keeps the illusory feeling of his/her limb and that of the environment through it.

To grow, or rather to mature, which means to set out on the path of transformation, implies to free oneself from this illusion through an opposite process: disillusionment. We have to underline the vital importance of linking these two reverse processes: that the mother—with the co-operation of the father and of other adults—

has first allowed the initial illusion[3] is as essential as the capacity offered to the child and to the mother to get rid of it.

Rose Fitzgerald Kennedy represents a figurehead of such an attitude towards her children; it led one of her sons to Presidency of the United States and two others to Senator Mandates. Do we have also to see here an explanation of the violent deaths of three of her sons, among whom are the President and one of the Senators? Opposed to that, one has to notice that some writers, notably F. Mauriac and M. del Castillo, bring forward examples of traumas suffered by the child when his/her mother shies away from his/her illusion.

As soon as we were born, the illusion of being able to restore completeness marks each of us with a deep and primitive imprint: a matrix that, in its turn, will give birth to three major illusions: omnipotence, immortality, and omniscience . Each of us will have to confront these illusions at different moments in one's life, a sequential process that seems common to every culture and civilization.

It is really a matrix because each of these illusions is a particular shaping of the original illusion of completeness:

- completeness in the area of action, with the illusion of being able to do everything: the illusion of omnipotence;
- completeness in the area of time, with the illusion of being able to escape from death: the illusion of immortality;
- completeness in the area of knowledge, with the illusion that everything is known or, at least, knowable: the illusion of omniscience.

This succession of illusions forces us to live a corresponding succession of painful disillusionment processes:

- when the infant experiences the limits of his power over his/her mother to make her act accordingly to his/her will,
- when the child meets death for the first time,
- when the adolescent discovers that his/her parents' knowledge, particularly his/her father's knowledge, is limited.

In each of these processes, the illusion helps to contain anxiety until the individual can confront the realty of reality, or better, the reality of the real. This creates a temporary transitional space adequate for the development and transformation of the being. But maintained for too long, it stops the exposure of each of us to the environment and to others: becoming antagonistic to this growth and this transformation. Whoever locks oneself in this illusion is doomed to make repetition his/her essential behaviour.[4] That's because, whatever avatar[5] it takes, the cause and the consequence—with a systemic effect—of the illusion of completeness is to negate the experience of lack. Doing this denies us access to the most powerful feeling that lack generates in us: desire. Desire can be encountered only through accepting incompleteness and lack.

None of us can escape going through these major illusions. Each of us has to experience them and then, in the best scenario, acknowledge, accept, and transform them through a process of disillusionment. This alternating, erratic, zigzagging process—illusion/disillusionment—offers us opportunities to construct ourselves continuously, to stop existing under the stronghold of our "systems-in-the-mind",[6] to gain a little freedom.

From this perspective, the illusion of the illusion would be to claim to be free from every illusion; this would be to deny this alternating movement that constructs us as both a human and a social being.

Moreover, the illusion of completeness also pushes us to believe we can completely control our thoughts, words and acts . . . a way of denying the unconscious, this radically Other who is also I. We are never complete because each of us, individually and collectively, has, of course, a conscious life, but also an unconscious life that he/she can know and acknowledge, in the best case, only partially, and then only from time to time.

One can also observe the print of this illusion at both a collective and systemic level: the illusion of completeness of the world. This underlies the myths that pretend to be "completely" explicative of the origin,[7] of past, present and future. These myths deny history: gods and heroes have already written it; human beings cannot find any place to be actors, and still less authors; it is the end of history (cf. Fukuyama, F., *The End of History and the Last Man*, Free Press, 1992).

In the political sphere, this illusion produces totalitarianism, which above all is, as the word reveals it, THE denial of incompleteness. The totalitarian society is, of course, a society without opposition but, above all, it is a society that tolerates neither difference nor deviance, nor surprise; a society of "sames", of clones— "xeroxization" instead of eroticization—and consequently a society practising ethnic cleansing. It is a society in which power is necessarily concentrated in the hands of a tyrant omnipresent—everywhere and nowhere as God . . . and the unconscious—through statues (35,000 statues of the North Korean dictator Kim Song il!), photos, paintings, and even doubles (cf. Saddam Hussein). It is a society where power pretends to know everything and to control every public and private activity.

Acceptance of incompleteness is the *sine qua non* condition of democracy: acceptance of the Other as different, radically different. This means without the possibility of comparing himself/ herself in comparison to me . . . including the way he/she imagines democracy!

The way we live out our feeling of incompleteness shapes our relationship toward the other: through a projection process it determines the way we consider him/her and what we expect from him/her.

Three possibilities are offered to us:

The first possibility: the encountering of the Other is the search for the complement that will, at least partly, restore our completeness. In this scenario, our life comes down to the endless quest for an illusory fusion.

As mentioned earlier, the experience of the initial separation with the mother is at the source of this illusion. However, it can be reactivated and implemented by the intense but ephemeral experience of gift and surrender in an encounter. The archetype of this experience is, of course, the amorous encounter. One can also feel it in experiencing co-operation in a task between two persons or two subsystems. It is not the joy and the creative power that such an experience generates that is illusory and trapping, rather it is the plan to perpetuate such ephemeral moments instead of renewing the experience by recreating them within successive "here and now"s.

Pretending to perpetuate the moment—projection rather than plan—implies the denial of reality, the reality of time, the reality of third parties, the reality of the Other,[8] and in the end the reality of oneself. It leads to locking oneself into almost autistic behaviour.

There is an important variant of this fusion, between both individuals and sub-systems. Here the other is not an allied complement but an enemy complement. Gradually, this enemy becomes essential as one exchanges pain in a system locked in on itself, covering every *raison d'être*. This situation can be met between persons (e.g. the couple of French writers Elise and Marcel Jouhandeau) and between sub-systems as well (e.g. the conflict between Israeli and Palestinians today).

Whether it is a fusion between allies or between enemies, the closure of the fusional system can only be broken by the eruption of a third party. Homeostasis of such a system can be so strong that this eruption frequently requires violence. At the beginning of life, this is the role of the father, who, by breaking the "fusional" link between the mother and the child (by enacting the "symbolic castration") prevents his/her "imaginary castration" and "authorizes" his/her existence.[9,10]

The second possibility: one acknowledges his/her own incompleteness but the resulting pain and guilt leads to *the search for another being, perfect because complete, inhuman because superhuman, who we will just have to venerate in order to anaesthetize our pain*. This attitude pushes the other into the role of an object rather than a subject. While dissolving oneself into the venerated object, one consciously or unconsciously attempts to deny or to silence one's own desires and lacks.

In that perspective, the extreme scenario is the quest of an expected Saviour or the veneration of an already come Saviour. Through sinking into the perfection of this Saviour, one attempts to go beyond one's incompleteness and to make it painless.

This dynamic frequently underlies some kinds of religious belief[11] but it can also be met in organizational life.

The quest for a mythic saviour or the "messianization"[12] of an actual individual has the effect—and the unconscious aim—of allowing offloading on to him/her, at least temporarily, the pain of the human condition and of its transformation. This dynamic underlies the success of several sects and of their chiefs.

This installs the vicious spiral "Saviour → Persecutor → Victim", at the end of which the venerated object, turned into a scapegoat, is immolated in order to make him/her expiate the inescapable failure of such a step and the incompleteness we have projected on him/her. This is probably why some leaders of sects push their disciples, with or without them, to collective suicide.

The third possibility and, in our view, *a unique way to completely live out our human and social condition: the acceptance of the Other as another Human Being, incomplete as well, with whom we can, by dialogue, live out the lack.* This is the condition for sharing feelings and desires inspired by this lack and, possibly, sublimating the lack at the risk of hybridization through a cross-fertilization.[13] Nevertheless, sublimation of the lack remains a possibility, not a guarantee.

Unlike the "fusional" quest where one considers the Other only by reference to oneself, as a complement, here, the Other is acknowledged and encountered for him/her self, as the incarnation of a radical otherness.

The encounter with this Other allows the setting up of a dialectical relationship. In the best cases, thanks to this relationship, each protagonist will have the opportunity to understand oneself a little bit more, to meet the Other within himself/herself and to travel through a stage of his/her own transformation the outcome of which is uncertain, indefinite, incomplete by definition. A travel that can be interrupted only by death.

This is the *dialogue of lacks*, "the secret core of dialogue", the Martin Buber's "Besod' Siach". This is the name of a Jewish prayer but also the name and the primary task of a friendly Israeli association.

Here, as usual, one can see the revealing strength of etymology. Etymology of the word "dialogue" strengthens our hypothesis about the "real" dialogue.

Dialogue comes from Greek words *dia* (δια) and *logos* (λογοσ).

Logos is the word, as means of expression but also as an opportunity to distance from the fact, from the event, from the experience.

The prefix *dia* indicates what distinguishes, what separates, but also "by", "by means of", and even, "across", "what goes through", "what prolongs". One can find it in diameter, measurement across, diachronic, across the time, but also diaspora: what prolongs by being disseminated in the space.[14] As Andre Chouraqui noted—in converse with Martin Buber, who considered the dyad as the place for dialogue above all else—dialogue does not mean "to talk in pair" as one usually thinks; it means to participate in a conversation, in pair or with several persons, with the aim of walking together toward the logos.

So, obviously, we have to promote dialogue, but surely not in order to search a complement, neither to offload on the other the guilt of our incompleteness, nor to project on him/her our repressed feelings and desires![15]

Dialogue, but dialogue of lacks, is the acknowledgement and sharing of the experience of emptiness, in order to provide each one, the other as well as my-self, with the opportunity not to fill the irreparable loss but to transform it.

Let us develop this dialogue, the dialogue that acknowledges desire, my own desire and the desire of the Other, the others. Difficult dialogue, unskilful dialogue groping its way through obstacles, often disappointing and depressing . . . but dialogue that summons up self-respect and respect for the Other, individual and collective, which makes possible the escape from the influence of our unconscious mental representations—the internal prison of the system in the mind—and allows surprise, which authorizes innovation and creation, which feeds life.

Notes

1. In this form, the word "dialogue" occurs twenty-one times in Jacques Chirac's talk, during the televised interview the President of French Republic gave on the occasion of Bastille Day, on 14 July 2003.
2. Note the word "fullness" or the expression "to be filled with joy" to designate some kinds of happiness.
3. "A mother's adaptation to the needs of her infant, when that mother is 'good enough', gives the infant the illusion that an external reality does exist that matches his own capacity to create". (D. W. Winnicott (1953), *Transitional Objects and Transitional Phenomena, A Study of the First Not-me Possession*).
4. For some authors, the fact that women are "generative of immortality" could constitute a handicap to having access to the creative and incentive power of illusions. It's notably the thesis of Nancy Huston, a Canadian novelist, that women who can, through motherhood, experience involvement in the succession of generations, feel less than men the need to perpetuate their stay on Earth by creating other works.

5. Let us remember that the word *avatar* comes from Sanskrit *avatara* meaning "descent". In religious vocabulary, avatars are successive incarnations of Vishnu "intending to restore cosmic and moral order after it has been disturbed by diabolical powers" (*Encyclopaedia Universalis*—"avatara").

6. Here is a possible definition of system-in-the-mind (SIM). SIM is the systemic construction—the system—through which every individual represents, in an unconscious way if it is not worked through, his environment. This construction at least influences—but often determines—his relationships, his behaviour, his decisions, his vision of himself and his place in the universe. SIM comes directly from the person's history and his relationships with his original institutions (family, school, etc.). It structures the individual and conditions his relationships with institutions in the here and now.

7. Every civilization has a myth describing the origin but, in spite what they claim, every myth leaves a gap, a hole at the origin of the origin, at the beginning of the beginning, . . . including the "big bang" theory!

8. In that sense that he/she is just considered as a complement, without having existence by him/her self

9. Existence comes from Latin *ex-ire*: to leave in order to go

10. An Indian proverb says: "The mother shows you who you are; the father shows you the world".

11. Very early Christian theology (*Origène*) criticized applying this representation to Jesus Christ because it would have led to considering Him as an "impassive" being, that is to say, spared human pain.

12. Confer the "Messie(r) nization" at Vivendi Universal . . . "The Universal Life", a significant conscious and unconscious choice, so significant!

13. We feel in syntonism with the editorial of Favilla, in the French paper "Les Echos" on 26 September 2003, entitled "Devastating dialogue". Referring to the definition of dialogue by Platoon, he writes:

[dialogue] is before all, for Greeks, a sharing with an uncertain outcome. [. . .]. [Its] first function is destroying illusory justifications, blowing up contradictions [. . .] Its main quality [is] to be an opportunity for shaking those who wanted to mutually convince themselves and so, to sketch the possibility of a surpassing. [. . .] This devastating dialogue explains the fear it provokes [because] according to Carl Rogers "the risk of being changed is one of the most frightening perspectives one can imagine".

14. One can also evoke "diaphragm" = across the partition, "diagram" = through, beyond the drawing, "diagnosis" = beyond the perception, the symptom . . . but also and above all "diabolic", which proves to be the opposite of "symbolic". Etymologically, the Greek word σθμβολον (*sumbolon*) designates the piece of wood divided between two persons in order to serve as a sign of recognition. It is what gathers together and allows sharing. In that perspective, diabolic is what prevents mutual recognition and forbids sharing.

15. On that point see the work of Ami Farago-Goffer, member of the Israeli association Besod' Siach.

POSTSCRIPT

Difficult dialogues: reflections on the journey of living

Faith Gabelnick

Introduction

In their essays, "Disillusionment" and "Dialogue of Lacks", Dr David Gutmann and his colleagues explore a complex hypothesis about the dialectical relationship between illusion and disillusion. This process can be also understood as the story of building one's identity and deepening one's understanding about life and death. The authors assert that this is not a linear process, nor is its goal an ultimate, final understanding of the human condition. Rather, the construction and deconstruction of illusion (disillusionment) enable us to mature, to embrace life with desire and in that very embrace, to also experience its absence. "It is about understanding where the boundary lies between survival . . . and a life of desire and creation" ("Disillusionment", p. 35)

One cannot imagine a more profound subject or a more difficult one to explore, for in the very process of trying to understand and articulate this process we inevitably create the illusion that language can define the undefinable. Still, as we are "in life", we must create illusions or "working hypotheses". These are like stories, or ideas, or philosophical positions that guide us along many pathways. We cannot avoid this process unless we want to remain in one place, content with our definitions and customs. To me, this is a living death, to others it may be happiness and contentment. But moving out of the black box (*boîte noire*) into a more transparent and transformational environment (a glass box/*boîte de verre*) takes courage and the ability to mourn. In fact, it is this ability to encounter death and loss, to grieve, to mourn, and to continue that allows us to live more authentic lives.

What follows is a story of illusion and disillusionment and the transformations that occurred. This story connects my inner and outer lives and the intersection of the personal and the professional. It is offered as an illustration of one human being's journey in the hope that it may illuminate the stories of others and offer a possibility of deeper understanding about the complex processes of discernment.

When parents die

Early years as a university president

As CEO and president of Pacific University, I would prepare at the beginning of each school year a State of the University Address to be delivered to the faculty, staff, and students. During the first few years, I spoke to the community about issues of institutional identity and being members of a learning community. I emphasized that our task was to reach towards new understandings about our relationships with one another as members of departments and divisions and about acknowledging our interdependence upon one another for the success of the whole community. I spoke about the importance of recognizing and honouring the vulnerability of the learner and the leader and emphasized that we grow when we learn from mistakes that inevitably occur when one takes risks. I invited all to think of themselves as learners and leaders and to join together in a common task of building the university community. People listened politely, applauded, and left.

Holding the illusions of omnipotence and omniscience, I conveyed my unwavering belief that my words and my personal passion and commitment could transform their internal mental models of university life and their own assessment of their authority to work and lead in that environment. I worked tirelessly to be a good mother-president by providing examples and strategies for the community to enable them to engage in a transformational process. They obediently formed cross-departmental work groups; they read materials I provided and attended workshops about institutional transformation, but they lacked desire and passion. They were passive and dependent—smiling through their anger and resentment of this all-powerful, too confident, and intrusive woman.

We were stuck, each in our own ways, in our own illusions. The harder I worked, the more people felt tired and under-appreciated. The mental model of institutional happiness and success that many held was focused on individual resources, on personal gain and recognition, not on the process of yielding some individual needs to benefit the entire community. People did not want to give up any of their territory, or even mourn the loss of their desire to be at a more endowed university. We were a financially poor university and people were focused on the lacks. The more I focused on the potential "wealth" of the community, the poorer everyone seemed to feel. I appeared to hold the hope, the optimism for transformation, but also would not acknowledge my role in this stagnation.

Middle years

This situation began to reach a crisis during the third year of my presidency. There was much unrest among the faculty, mainly because our enrolments were not increasing, salaries were still low, and additional financial resources were not coming in to the university. A feeling of impoverishment was everywhere. I dismissed this feeling as an illusion; they experienced it as Reality. We were all stuck in the black box. How we moved out of the black box was a process of zigs and zags—uneven, totally unpredictable, but profound.

During that third year, we applied, at my intense urging and with strong leadership from my senior staff and a few senior faculty members, for two major foundation grants, one to support research for the undergraduate faculty and their students and one to support interdisciplinary faculty—generated projects around experiential

learning that would link the graduate faculty with the undergraduate faculty, as well as staff members and community pro-
grammes. Faculty came to me to say that it was folly to apply to
these prestigious foundations, that we, as a university, lacked a
unifying vision, that we did not have research projects that were
worthy of funding. Still, I persisted: people were invited to form
work groups, and as they met in dialogue to discuss their ideas,
their creativity and desire were ignited.

To my surprise, I discovered that whenever I offered my ideas I
was pushed away, like an intruding mother. Faculty became the
leaders of both grant efforts, and they began to take charge and
tentatively speak about possibilities for transformation. Ideas
flowed; new relationships were formed within the university; and
a unifying vision (or working hypothesis) of a university that
focused on learning through experience began to take shape in their
minds and hearts. As they pushed me away from the working
sessions, I began to feel freer to focus on other aspects of the university that involved fund-raising and administrative structures. I also
began to shift away from the role of overbearing, overly knowl-
edgeable, maternal president. The grants became a transitional
object or perhaps a transitional process to enable a different kind of
identification with the university (and, ultimately, with its president) to occur. Both of these grants were submitted in the spring of
1998, and we were to be notified in the summer of that year about
whether or not we would receive funding.

Simultaneously, in my personal life, other events, equally difficult, were occurring. In the winter of this third year, my mother had
a virulent recurrence of breast cancer. I felt as if I had been hit in the
very core of my being, bent over by the realization of the imminent
death of my mother. While the campus was in the throes of
wrestling with its identity and its own confidence to transform
itself, I was also now embroiled in a parallel process with my relationship to my mother. In April, as the grants were being finalized,
my mother went into the hospital as the cancer had spread to her
brain, eliminating her ability to speak, among other functions. On
campus, in addition to the grant-writing processes, the graduate
professional faculty were roiling about wanting higher compensation, enrolments still continued to drift, and my senior staff was not
working as a team. My time was spent between attending to this

needy, dissatisfied campus and flying across the US to be with my mother. I remember taking a telephone call from mother's physician saying she had maybe a month to live and then walking directly into a group of faculty who were arguing for my support for their compensation. Everyone was grieving and in a state of need. We all wanted to be taken care of by the Good Mother, and we all were encountering lacks.

My mother died at the end of May—a week after the formal end of the school year. Before leaving the campus to be with my mother, I presided over the graduation ceremonies. We call the ending ceremony of a university both a "Commencement" and a "Graduation", a beginning and an end. Thus, it was for me. Young people were graduating with their new hopes and illusions and desires, and their parents were moving into their mid-lives, encountering the deaths of their parents and their own mortality. We represented, as in a tableau, the many phases of life. Some had already stepped out of the black box and lived in a clearer light; others clung to their old patterns and ideas. Yet we could not avoid the acknowledgement of the ultimate fact of human existence. Completing this tumultuous academic year, I flew to the East Coast to be with my mother in her final days.

A week later, when I gave the eulogy for my mother, I said that her death had left a hole in my heart, that there was a silence, a quietness that I would always carry. I said that my mother and I did not agree on most things, that at some level I did not understand her. What I carried forth, however, was her joy of living, her engagement with the community, her devotion (in her own way) to her family. As I spoke, I dispelled many illusions that people had about me and about my relationship with my mother. I spoke frankly, strongly, with humour and love. My mother was a woman who loved tradition and predictability; she was formally religious and gave herself tirelessly to Jewish philanthropies; yet she produced this daughter who was a Feminist, an Atheist, who pursued a full-time profession as she raised her children and would not stay home to cook the Sabbath meal. This first daughter, named Faith, endlessly challenged her mother's faith, warring against what she saw as her mother's illusions and, unconsciously, creating her own illusions of her omnipotence, immortality, and omniscience.

In June, the month of my birth, my exhaustion was so intense that I began to have panic attacks. As I slept and dreamed and reorientated myself to the new reality of my mortality and my responsibility as an institutional and family leader, I realized that the gift of my mother's death was a release of me for being the torch bearer of other's illusions. I realized how much I was like my mother—wanting to marshall people around my vision, to make them believers in my own form of religion. My mother was a great illusionist. In her presence I was never quite sure of what the facts or "reality" of a particular situation was, so filtered was it by her intransigent views of the world. In so many ways, she was inaccessible, surrounded, protected by her passionate illusions—as perhaps I was to the campus. As I dreamed and meditated and grieved, I began to feel more calm, more centred. I knew I needed to individuate yet another time from my mother, even though she had died. I knew that I had to take up my roles, public and private, in different ways. I began to understand that despite my outer rebellions, I continued to be the Good Daughter and that my unconscious obedience was preventing transformation because it was so filled with anger towards this mother who had been so unavailable. These feelings mirrored a similar anger and resistance that I had been encountering on campus.

At the end of June (almost exactly on my birthday), I understood that the university's structure and many of the personnel would have to change. We would grieve their loss, but we would then be able to move on. With great trepidation, I released two senior administrators and reorganized the academic administrative structure of the university. Others left soon after, and by the end of the summer, while we were conducting searches for four major senior positions, I was building a new, collaborative team consisting of all the deans and directors, helping them to learn how to share information and work more openly with one another. They began to develop more trust among themselves, releasing a little of their territorial mentality so that we could all understand our finances and our needs as a university. As my unconscious resistances to my internal authority figures loosened, so did others to me. When I appointed interim senior officials from the faculty ranks after consultation with many of these faculty, nods of approval were seen, and when we began these senior searches and encountered some challenges, people came up to me and said, "Don't settle for second-best. Hire the best available". As new people accepted these prestigious positions and began to take up their roles, the campus seemed to feel more confident. Their president was doing a better job of delegating and acknowledging the competencies of others. (It is interesting to note that one of the strong legacies for which I received great appreciation when I retired has been the creation of the strongest team of senior managers the university has ever had.)

In mid-summer, we received word from the two foundations that both of the grants, totalling more than half a million dollars, had been approved for Pacific University. The campus was in disbelief, but the transformation was now under way. We had received external confirmation about our potential as researchers and as excellent teachers, and we had put in place the leadership teams to help us examine our processes and to lead us in the many difficult dialogues that would inevitably face us.

Final years

My State of the University Address that autumn talked about the transformational power of Surprise. That theme—the ability to be surprised, which I linked with desire, and the acknowledgement of loss or disappointment—continued throughout the remainder of my presidency. Each subsequent year new events happened that we had never expected: some were wonderful; others were awful or tragic. People still listened, applauded, and left, but the atmosphere in the large hall had changed, and I had changed. As I spoke, the audience was listening to their own accomplishments, remembering and acknowledging their own and their colleagues' disappointments, celebrating their dreams and the many unexpected events—joys and sorrows—that were truly the fabric of this community. As I matured, as I relinquished—to some degree—my own illusions of omnipotence and omniscience, there was a space created for others to risk, to desire, to fail, to celebrate. As my internal world shifted, this university community shifted—not in a perfect way—but in a way that allowed some new experiences and therefore some new learning.

In a small university community, there are no secrets. We are inside one another; we know each other. The last years of my presidency were almost as tumultuous as some of the middle years. After September 11, the stock market fell, enrolments that had soared began to fall, and financial problems challenged us again. The anxiety on campus about the future was projected on to the financial health of the university and on its president. But this president was now more experienced; she was bringing in financial resources, and community connections. We were a different institution, but the old visions of deprivation began again to surface.

In the seventh year of my presidency, in late October, my father developed metastatic lung cancer that went to his brain. After much family consultation, we brought my father to live with us for his remaining months. It was a year of deaths: my mentor, my cousin, my step-son, my former mother-in-law, my uncle—as well as tragic deaths of students and community residents. My father remained alert until his final weeks and talked to me about the challenges I was facing as a university president. As a former CEO of a small company, he was very proud of his daughter, and I now felt very connected to him, consciously and unconsciously. I accompanied him on his last journey, but it was my husband who cared for him daily. He called my husband "his brother", and I called my husband my angel and protector. My father was a practical and frank man, gregarious, artistic—under-appreciated by his family. He had his own illusions, but they were less intransigent than my mother's and I felt that I could reach into him and have a dialogue. He didn't agree with me very often, but he listened as I argued in my usual passionate way. He hated being in Oregon, ripped away from his home, dependent upon us. He did not want to die.

When my father died in the early spring, almost exactly four years after my mother's death, the gift and release came again. I was now a grandmother of one granddaughter, with another one to be born later that year. My immediate family, long put aside on behalf of my professional life, called to me. I realized that when my last parent died, I no longer was driven to fulfil their dreams and desires. I needed to find ways of taking up these new roles of grandmother and matriarch, and I wanted to create a professional life more free of institutional demands. Yet I was locked in the illusion of indispensability. I thought that I needed to stay as president for a few more years to lead the campus through (yet another) crisis. I went through a brief depression and a revelation. Again, with trepidation but also a new clarity and calm, I announced to the community in May 2002 that I would retire as president in sixteen months.

My State of the University Address that year spoke about my role as Transitional Leader. While some were pleased by my announcement, the majority, on campus and in the community, were uneasy or dismayed. They did not want this change at this time, but as I spoke, I talked from my heart about the new desire I felt to live in a different way, and I asked them to support me in this journey. I reminded them that they knew about loss and change from their own experiences, and I recounted some of my own experiences around this connection and loss and transition. I outlined a succession plan and asked them to join me in making it successful. This time the community rose in a standing ovation, full of confidence for themselves and appreciation of the time to prepare for this transition. Faculties, administrators, trustees, all made separate declarations to support this transitional year, and during those two years we raised more money than ever in the history of the university. The enrolments, when I stepped down, were the highest in decades. My successor was someone who would continue much of what we had begun, and we worked together to effect a seamless transition.

At one of the many farewell ceremonies prepared for me by the university and the community, we moved the oldest building on campus from a sheltered place deep within the campus to a prominent site at the edge of campus across the street from the Congregational Church, whose elders had founded the university and erected this building. My farewell speech was delivered as the building was moved to its new foundation. There was something wonderfully symbolic and congruent about moving a building. We think there are so many things—including buildings—that are immovable; and yet desire and imagination, respect for a community and connection to the past, enable all types of transformation. People exclaimed that the building looked so much bigger in its new location, more august, more prominent, taking up its own authority as both a symbol of the origin of the university and beacon for its future. And so it seemed to me. It was a surprise!—a wonderful surprise for all of us. A sequoia tree, with a tribute to me, is planted now near the building. It will reach towards the skies in the years beyond our lives and hold aloft the promise of new growth.

Concluding reflections

I often wonder whether it is more the literal rather than the figurative death of our parents that offers such great gifts to us as children. We speak rather glibly, I think, about separation/individuation issues and about the inherent anxieties accompanying the trauma and necessity of that separation process. And we actually spend our lives creating transitional or permanent illusions to enable us to live with the memory of the lost world of the womb or the imagined triumph of our hearts and minds over our parents' powerful influences. However, in my experience I have found that until there is a finality, an end to the lived journey, we still hold on to some of our illusions. At some level, while our parents are alive, we are always the children; we are always on the journey of illusion/disillusion, re-enacting and then realizing the many transitional illusions we have developed over the years. We are always struggling for attention, to show how competent we are, to be great lovers and lock ourselves in the old embrace that we remember so well—the holding and the gaze of unconditional love. And we are always caught between Thanatos and Eros, in the passage of life, dying a bit each day, even as we cherish the sunlight.

I am at a stage in my life where I am a close observer of the beginning and the end of this cycle. I have watched the first moments of my granddaughters' latching on to their mother's breast, and I have seen, as their eyesight improved, the loving gaze of the infant toward the mother. This gaze is the manifestation of attachment, of the illusion of a new union outside of the womb, and I know, as we all know, that the gaze will stray, that the mother will necessarily distance herself, that the child will walk away, and that the parents will struggle and compete for that gaze. Living and dying are partners. We embrace both or we stay blind to the possibilities of creativity.

I learned as president that my internal life permeated everything I did. My community felt it, and they contributed their own internal experiences to build a complex way of working together. However, the unexpected deaths of my parents during my presidency allowed me to become wiser and more flexible, to make decisions I thought that I could not make, to see into the Heart of Darkness and not be afraid. Tasting the Forbidden Fruit is always an opportunity to learn, but instead of leading to the Promised Land, this tasting of knowledge can lead to Lands of Promise. This is the journey of living and dying. I have learned to love this journey.